Noon, With a View

"… a great friend … thank you for the good work you do …" *Tony Blair*

"Sir Noon – a philanthropist – one of our prominent community members." *His Holiness Dr Mohammad Burhanuddin, spiritual leader of the Bohra community*

"A great leader for moderate Muslim thought…" *John Gummer, MP*

"A great contributor to our country." *Prime Minister Gordon Brown*

"… a man of total integrity…" *from the Foreword by Lord Sainsbury*

"An inspiring autobiography of a self-made man who rose from humble origins to untold wealth. Noon made invaluable contributions to the development of the land of his birth (India) and the land of his adoption – England." *Khushwant Singh Iconic Editor, author & Journalist of India*

"This finely written and deeply moving book narrates the remarkable life of a man who rose from humble origins to become one of the most respected and admired individuals in Britain and India. His courage, determination, integrity, and moral transparency shine through the book. Sir Gulam draws strength from misfortunes and tragedies, turns them into opportunities, and shows that worldly success need not involve compromise with one's conscience and deeply held convictions." *Professor Lord Parekh*

NOON, WITH A VIEW
Courage and Integrity

Sir Gulam Noon, MBE, NDI

Whittles Publishing

Published by
Whittles Publishing Ltd.,
Dunbeath, Caithness, KW6 6EY,
Scotland, UK
www.whittlespublishing.com

ISBN 1-904445-79-1

Printed by Bell and Bain Ltd., Glasgow

I would like to dedicate this book to my mother,
Bilkis Safiabai Kaderbhai Mithaiwalla,
who is the inspiration of everything I do,
and my father, Kaderbhai Ebrahamjee,
who died when I was very young

ACKNOWLEDGEMENTS

All my family members are precious to me and I should thank them all for making me so proud: my special thanks to my wife, Mohini, for her love and support. She is the one who has also spent long hours with me shaping my thoughts as I wrote this book and my thanks to her parents, Amrit and Patty Kent for all their many kindnesses to me over the years.

My thanks to my brothers, Abbas and Akbar and their wives, Rehana and Josette; my sisters, Atekaben, Shirin and Kaniz, and my brothers-in-law, Moiz and Fakri; my daughters, Zeenat and Zarmin, my sons-in-law, Arun and Manraj, my granddaughter, Natania and my nephews and nieces: Nizar, Naeem, Zahid, Firoz, Alexi, Mikael, Aamir, Aziz, Ibrahim, Nazaneen, Shamin, Mubina and Shamina. I should also like to mention their spouses: Samina, Purnima, Ruxana, Salma, Nisrin, Fatima, Aslam, Anees, Mohammed and Akhtar. Similarly my grand-niece Nusrat and nephew Hussain, who reside in Dubai and Hani and Kamil who are both studying in the USA.

Every one of them and all my friends, too many to mention by name but they know who they are, have all knowingly and unknowingly played an important part in my life.

And finally, I must thank Bob Whittington, who has worked with me on this book, travelled with me to my hometown in Rajasthan to help me put my experiences and thoughts into words; and Keith Whittles, my long suffering publisher who has put up with delays in getting the final manuscript as I tried to juggle writing with business.

CONTENTS

PREFACE

The prime motive for writing an autobiography must surely be to record events which otherwise will be lost to posterity. For me there is pride; pride in my family, my work and my colleagues, pride in my hometown and my adopted home. I hope that the sons and daughters who are studying now in my old local schools in Sunel and Bhawani Mandi in India will be inspired to go on to achieve even greater things, travel the world, build great businesses and strong families of their own and yet be able to remember with humility and gratitude, and with the same pride that I enjoy, where they came from.

My only concern in writing such a book is that I will not have listed every event, every kindness and every individual who has enabled me to get through my life so far; some events I have simply forgotten and for that I am sorry; others are best left unsaid. It is futile to seek revenge for wrongs or try to settle scores in such a work just as it is in life; however, it is right to put the record straight and to ensure that future generations understand why I did certain things and, possibly, avoid the same mistakes.

My desire, the fire in my belly which continues to burn, has been to achieve everything that I possibly could with whatever talents and support I have been fortunate to enjoy. I have no other agenda or motive. I am a businessman but I will always fight for what I believe is right and defend the defenceless in whatever field I am working, be it business, education, health or welfare.

I hope there is something for everyone in this story: encouragement, advice, inspiration or simply just a little background about a boy who had a dream and a conviction that there was more to life than what was laid out before him.

To those who feel I have let them down in some way in the past, please accept my apologies; for those whom I have been able to help in some way, please multiply what you have received by what you can do for others; for my family and friends in fast moving cities around the world or the calm of Bhawani Mandi and Sunel in Rajasthan, thank you.

Gulam Noon

New Labour came into power in 1997 determined to create a society which was built on both enterprise and social justice, and Tony Blair was personally committed to gaining the support of people who had been successful but who also wanted to live in a fair society. I was, therefore, delighted when Gulam Noon became a supporter of the party, as I knew him to be both a highly successful entrepreneur and a man with a social conscience.

I had first met him in 1989 when he came to Sainsbury's to try to persuade us to buy his chilled Indian meals. It was obvious from the moment he entered the room that here was a man who not only knew his business extremely well but who also shared our passion for food, and over the years he became one of our best and most innovative suppliers.

A visit to one of his factories was always a great pleasure, and this was not only because it usually ended with a delicious Indian meal. His passion for quality and his production skills enabled him to produce traditional Indian food, with its emphasis on fresh ingredients, on a factory-level scale, and the dedication of his staff was incredibly impressive. And if you want to know how great entrepreneurs act in adversity read how he rebuilt his business after it was devastated by fire.

I am glad that in this book he has decided to tell his side of the 'Cash for Honours' story. Anyone who has met him knows that he is a man of total integrity who is enormously well respected in his community, and the way that he was treated at this time is not something we can be proud of as a country.

This is the exciting story of a born entrepreneur who started with a single small sweet shop in Mumbai in India and became the head of a highly successful food empire, and I hope that many young people will read it and be inspired both to create successful, high-quality manufacturing businesses and to make a lasting contribution to their communities, as he has done.

Lord Sainsbury of Turville

Chapter One

WEDNESDAY 22 MARCH 2006,
NUMBER 10 DOWNING STREET, LONDON

I should not have lost my temper but the frustration, the anger and the sense of betrayal had got the better of me. I had quite literally screamed at Ruth Turner, the Director of Government Relations and keeper of Tony Blair's Diary, the day before. I had demanded to see someone. With me were two close friends, Lord Waheed Alli and Baroness Margaret McDonagh – I suspect that they would not have come if they had realised what I was planning to say!

I had become deeply embroiled in the so-called Cash for Honours inquiry – the name given to the storm alleging a link between political donations and the promise of a peerage. My name had been dragged through the mud, my reputation was in danger of being ruined and none of it was my fault. I told Ruth that when I had agreed for my name to go forward I had openly declared all my donations to the Labour Party. I had filled in the appropriate form listing my financial dealings with the party – as Lord Levy, the chief fund raiser, knew. Why was I now facing a police investigation? Was this how loyalty to the party was rewarded? What was the Prime Minister going to do about it? How was he going to get me out of this mess?

I am sure some of my language might have been stronger but the message was plain enough. I was being hung out to dry. I should have been supported publicly by the most powerful people in the land; instead I was being investigated for political manipulation. As far as the public, my friends and my business acquaintances around the world were concerned, where there was smoke there must have been fire. People far away in places such as India and the Middle East who are not familiar with the British political system are still confused about what happened. Even after all the coverage in the western media, an editor of a major news magazine in Delhi asked me to explain what had transpired.

Ruth did her best to calm me down. It was not her fault and she too was in the firing line, but I had had enough of the rumour and innuendo, and someone had to hear my grievances. I had maintained complete silence despite persistent calls from the press all eager to publish my account. They smelled blood, and anything that would add to the story, particularly if it moved the line of inquiry closer to Number 10, was more than welcome.

Ruth was sure everything would be sorted out. She thought I might be found a safe seat as an MP, but I said I was not interested; I had even withdrawn my name from the list of potential peers. But I still wanted satisfaction. That was why the next day I found myself sitting in Downing Street waiting to meet Tony Blair.

This was not a new experience for me. As a long-time and open supporter of the Labour Party, as well as a high-profile member of the Asian community, I had attended many functions in Downing Street, but this time it was different. I was still struggling to control my temper and I did not want to say anything I might later regret. It was a particularly important meeting for me and on a very sensitive issue. To be honest, I did not know what I was going to say. Although I regarded him as a friend, Tony Blair was still the Prime Minister, the most important political figure in the land, and you did not just walk into Downing Street and give the Prime Minister a telling off. But I was genuinely worried.

Was this how it was all going to end after so many years spent building a successful business in the UK, making many friends, being honoured and knighted by the Queen? What about my family? What about my business? Had I really struggled from a one-room flat in Mumbai to end up facing charges in a criminal court in England for something as grubby as trying to buy a favour? I had been the youngest Justice of the Peace back in Mumbai. I had never in my life been questioned by the police, and never been involved in a court case in Britain let alone as a suspect, so this was a traumatic period. Everything I had done had been at the behest of the Labour Party and its senior officials. If honours were so cheap, people would be queuing up outside Downing Street, cheque books in hand. Surely everyone could see the absurdity of it all. The thought was scant comfort to me.

I looked around the room almost in a daze. I could hear the staff going about their business and the occasional sound from the world outside. It was like waiting outside the headmaster's study at school. Why was I feeling like the guilty party? I was convinced in my own mind that I had done nothing wrong. I checked my watch. He was running late, as it was Prime Minister's Questions in the House of Commons. Then just as my mind began wandering back to my business affairs, Tony Blair strode through the door, hand outstretched, apologising for keeping me waiting.

I immediately relaxed, his beaming smile working its magic on me as it had done on the electorate when his vision of "New Labour" gave him a landslide election victory over John Major's Conservatives in the 1997 general election. The Blair charm offensive was well known and it formed, in my view, a perfect combination with Gordon Brown's more austere public persona over at the Treasury.

He led me by the hand to his private apartment upstairs. His wife, Cherie, and their daughter, Kathryn, were there. Cherie greeted me with a kiss on the cheek and introduced Kathryn. To a casual observer it was an informal chat in a typical family context. Tony must have realised the tension and he used the informality of his sitting room to calm me down; no doubt Ruth Turner had warned him about my mood. Cherie and Kathryn came and went; the Blairs' youngest son Leo's toys were lying around – absolute normality, like any other home. But we were there to discuss anything but a normal matter. We sat facing each other and he told me: "I am devastated about what has happened to you. We have treated you badly."

I said: "Prime Minister, I don't know what has been going on with this peerage business, but you have got to get me out of this mess. I am not interested in going to the House of Lords anymore; in fact I have withdrawn my name from the list."

His reply both comforted and flattered me: "Gulam, you may not want to go to the House of Lords, but I want to send you there."

We talked about the investigation as it affected me and about the impact it was having on my family. I explained that I was now also getting negative reactions from overseas, where I had friends and business associates who were bemused by the stories they were reading and hearing.

Throughout our short meeting he did his best to reassure me. Although he could not of course pass judgement at the time as the inquiry was still going on, he said that we were all honourable people and he was sure in his heart of hearts – as I was – that no one had done anything wrong. This helped, but the story that began in March 2006 was to rumble on until 20 July 2007 when the Crown Prosecution Service (CPS) finally decided that there were no grounds to charge anyone. All the accusations had been completely without foundation. The CPS concluded:

> There is furthermore substantial and reliable evidence that there were proper reasons for the inclusion of all those whose names appeared on the 2005 working peers list, or drafts of that list: that each was a credible candidate for a peerage, irrespective of any financial assistance that they had given, or might give, to the Labour Party.

I did not realise it at the time, but Tony Blair would himself be quizzed by the police in December 2006 and twice again later, making him the first sitting Prime Minister to be questioned by the police in a criminal investigation, albeit as a witness. Despite being concerned for myself, I could tell that Tony Blair was also a worried man. At stake were his future and the legacy he had fought for. The prospect of appearing as a witness at the Old Bailey – or worse, as the accused – must have caused him some sleepless nights. Eventually, of course, he would step down as Prime Minister, but to what extent did the phantom scandal hasten his departure?

Margaret McDonagh joined us briefly and helped Tony Blair to reassure me that all would be well. He urged me not to be downhearted about the affair. I took encouragement from the meeting. I was no longer angry but I was still concerned and would remain so until the CPS eventually threw out the case.

★ ★ ★

13 FEBRUARY 1946 – MUMBAI, INDIA

Typically, my mind was not on the subject. The temperature outside was climbing to the thirties, the temperature inside the crowded classroom much the same: thirty or forty boys crammed into one room with only open windows to keep us cool. This was The Central School in Mohammedali Road, Mumbai, which was on two floors of a building with a hospital on the top floor and shops below us. The teacher had failed to capture my attention, but then few of them did. I was not a star pupil; my mind even then was always distracted by other things. Surprisingly for a lad of ten, I was thinking in my own simple way about business. I could not wait to escape the books and the academic subjects, which to my mind were irrelevant. I could not see how I was going to be able to apply geography and history to my life, and there was only one thing to do – get out and start earning a living.

The town crier as usual was wandering through the streets outside with the latest bit of news. India in 1946 was a place of tension: the world's largest democracy was about to be born. There was rioting in the streets, and there would be more bloodshed – much of it in the name of religion. But politics was not my concern: that would come much later. I was just thinking about how much longer this lesson would continue.

I began to tune in to the town crier as he got closer. Something made me think that he was talking to me. Then I heard his cry: it was my father's name. My father had died. I was dumbstruck. I looked around but no one else seemed to realise and I did not have the courage to get up and leave. The teacher just carried on completely oblivious: after all, there was a death announcement like this every day and he was not to know that one of the young pupils sitting in front of him had just lost his father.

I had to endure another hour before I could leave, and then I ran all the way home. The first person I saw was my brother-in-law, Kutbuddin. He said how sorry he was as I brushed past him and ran up the three flights of stairs to our single-room flat. My mother was distraught. She sat there sobbing, with my father laid out before her in the middle of the room, at last free from his long illness – a combination of diabetes and heart problems. I remember her saying to him then: "Why have you left me with young children like this?" My sister, Kaniz, was just a babe in arms.

I do not know what made me say it, but standing in front of my father's body I made my mother a promise there and then: "Don't worry. When I grow up I will take care of everything." My eldest sister, Ateka, still remembers those words today. I do not even know how or why I said them, but I was convinced that somehow it would be my job to put things right.

Chapter Two

Origins and Family Roots

I was born on 24 January 1936 in Mumbai. I was the second of three sons and I also had three sisters. We lived in a small apartment close to the docks. We and our neighbours enjoyed a simple life – in fact you could describe it as basic, and a struggle for my mother with a large family to bring up. There was no proper furniture. Each night my mother would lay out mats on the floor for our beds, in a neat line along one wall; the cooking and washing area was at the other end of the room. But we had happiness in abundance and there was a strong bond between all the members of our family. When I took my granddaughter back to that room to see where her family had started, she couldn't help crying. It was so far removed from her life in London, almost too different to comprehend. She had so much with which to compare these very rudimentary surroundings, whereas for me at one time this was home and I knew nothing else. I had my family, my friends, and I did not go hungry. What more would a little boy crave? In fact it was the strength of this unity, typical of Indian Muslim families, that held us together when my father died.

I should explain the family structure first, which to western eyes at least might seem complicated and unusual. My uncle was Kamruddin Ebrahamjee, who started the family food business back in 1898. The sign over the door was simply his name – nothing flashy or catchy. "Kamruddin Ebrahamjee" was where every Muslim went to buy the sweets that Indians eat on every occasion: birth, deaths, marriages or any festivity. The move into curry had not even been imagined.

My grandfather, Ebrahamjee, had two sons: my father, Kaderbhai, and his elder brother, Kamruddin. My father married twice, as is Muslim practice; he had one son, Kalimuddin, and two daughters by his first marriage to Fatema, and three daughters and three sons from his second marriage to Safiabai, who was my mother. My mother had no other relatives in India, having come from Shiraz in Iran with her father at the age of nine. Her name at birth was Bilkis, which was changed at the time of her marriage according to tradition. Her Iranian friends continued to call her Bilkis.

My mother also married twice. She was the widow of my uncle, Kamruddin Ebrahamjee, with whom she had two children, Mohammed Husain and Fatima. A widow at twenty-four, a foreigner, good-looking, with two small children, she had to marry to survive. My father's family arranged for her to wed the younger brother, Kaderhboy. This is common practice, even today. My father married her no doubt for many reasons – among them duty and family honour. Strict principles of behaviour and moral values were drummed into us, and loyalty to our extended family was a given. It would have been inconceivable that my mother should have been abandoned to fend for herself.

Soon after the outbreak of World War II, my father, like many others at the time, decided to move his young family out of the city to the relative safety of his home town of Sunel in the Jhalawar district of Rajasthan State. Sunel was where my grandfather, my father and his elder brother were all born. However, I go back to Bhawani Mandi, where my uncle built a house in 1926 that is still occupied by us. Bhawani Mandi is about eight miles from Sunel. Life was more comfortable in the family home in Bhawani Mandi and the cost of living was low in comparison with that of living in the big city. In fact we were probably better off than most people. My roots with the area are strong and to this day I look forward to returning home every year to escape the stress of modern business life. There is a more normal and natural pace to everyday living in Bhawani Mandi. If you asked me whether I could ever live full time in India now, the answer would be no – not because I love India any less but because I have simply moved on. I have my businesses, my immediate family and so many other interests in England that it would just be impractical to run my life from India. Like many Indians who have come to settle in the UK, England is my true home now and has my loyalty, but India will always remain my motherland.

In those days the relatively short journey from Bhawani Mandi to Sunel was an adventure. We went by bullock cart – two bullocks to a cart, and four during the monsoons – and it was hard work wading through the river and rumbling through the jungle. In those days it took us five hours in the dry months and eight hours in wet weather. During the rainy season, when the river was overflowing, the only way across was by raft with four men swimming alongside guiding the raft to the other side, where another bullock cart awaited. We could so easily have been swept away, but I remember it all as a time of excitement with the wildlife following us on our slow and at times treacherous journey. Today, tarmacked roads, a bridge spanning the river and a modern car have cut the journey time down to twenty minutes.

There are no airs and graces in Bhawani Mandi and I treasure the moments I can spend there, sitting and sharing a meal with friends and neighbours regardless of their means, as my family have done for generations. Naturally they take an interest in what I am doing overseas and are amused whenever I crop up in the headlines. They all think that I must drink because I live in London and they wonder how I can socialise there without being a drinker and a smoker. They are also surprised that I still cook. I cook at home in London, and when I am in Bhawani Mandi I will also prepare a barbecue. I have always felt happiest working with the chefs and not sitting up in a grand management office giving orders. Riding your high horse or failing to keep your feet on the ground is the way to lose key people and destroy your business. Chefs are creators and artists and I like to be alongside them. A chef, of course, can be an angry man too because he works with fire all the time. They are like scientists – have you ever met a scientist with a rational mind?

The family was well established in the Sunel area to the extent that my father and uncle were able to build a small hospital for the community in

1925, which was opened by the local maharajah. This act of generosity was typical; whenever they could, my father and his brother showed their natural tendency to be philanthropic. The maharajah was so taken by the hospital that he asked them if they would build a second one in Bhawani Mandi. They said that they did not have enough money from their immediate resources but if the maharajah would lend them 40,000 rupees (about £500) they would undertake the project, and they offered the family bungalow as a mortgage or guarantee until the money was returned. But consider for a moment this act of kindness and selflessness: to mortgage your own property to build something for the community from which you stood to make no commercial gain – indeed potentially to put yourself at financial risk. It is humbling to think that there were, possibly still are, people like that in the world.

In later years my mother also had an opportunity to share her good fortune with others, no doubt remembering the hardships she herself had endured. Some time after my father's death, when our business had stabilised again, the local *tehsildar* (local government officer), Mr Mubarak Shah Khan, from Bhawani Mandi, took her to see some refugees living in makeshift tents. They were Hindu Sindhis from the province of Sindh, which had come from the newly formed country of Pakistan in the bloody Partition of 1947. Millions of people were displaced, losing their homes, property and in many cases their lives. These dispossessed families had escaped the holocaust and made their way to Bhawani Mandi. The *tehsildar* wanted to show my mother the conditions they were living in, thinking that my she might give some money for meals. At this time she was overseeing the construction of rooms that my father had started building before his death. These were modest buildings with 21 small apartments for rent, but I don't want to give the impression that my mother was a rich property dealer. When she saw the terrible state of the camp, my mother said without any hesitation to the *tehsildar*, "You choose twenty-one families and bring them here because I cannot bear to see them in the scorching sun." The collector said: "You cannot do that. They are unable to pay any rent." She said they would not have to pay anything. Later they paid a peppercorn rent of 15 rupees per month (about 15p).

Twenty-five years later my mother said to me, "I don't want you ever to displace these people." With my commercial hat on I said that property prices had risen and asked her what she would like me to do. She said: "I don't know, just make sure they are looked after." I decided that I would sell the houses to the families for 5000 rupees each on instalments. Of course that gave me problems with the tax man, who thought I was taking him for a fool by claiming to have sold the houses for 5000 rupees when they were worth ten times that amount. He assumed I had received money under the table. I thought the best solution was for my mother to tell the story in her own words to the commissioner, whose name was Mr Agarwal. In the end Mr Agarwal accepted her word with tears in his eyes. I was there. He said: "Lady, I believe you." Today there are third and fourth generations still living in those same homes. My opportunity to make a contribution to others' lives would come later, but I always say that I did not learn philanthropy from anyone: it is in my genes, which came from my father and mother.

I cannot stress enough the unity that held us together as a family. Although there were step-fathers and step-mothers, half-brothers and half-sisters among us, we never had any disharmony. That's the incredible part, which I suppose is partly down to the culture – we respected our elders, and one another, highly. We don't talk about cousins or step- this and that: they are our brothers and sisters. We were all there to help one another, although none of us was rich; no one was allowed to go hungry. The contrast between this way of life and that of today's rootless societies is vivid, although in India it still exists, particularly outside the big cities.

My father had great respect for his elder brother, Kamruddin, so much that when he came to build a bigger family home in Sunel he named it after him: "Kamar Manzil". This too was traditional. Even now my respect for my brother, Abbas, who is four years older than me, is enormous – I would not dream of confronting him in an argument, and even though on paper you could say I was more successful from a purely financial perspective, that is totally irrelevant. There has never been any jealousy between me and my brothers, Abbas and Akbar; in commercial and business matters they have always left the decisions to me and given me their full support. That respect would probably have been multiplied ten times over in the past, so it was perfectly normal to name buildings after elder brothers, fathers or grandfathers.

We moved back to Mumbai when I was eight because my father thought the business he had established in the city was suffering in his absence, but once again we could only afford a modest one-room flat. Gradually, as the business slowly prospered, we rented a second room across the hallway, and that is how we lived for most of my younger days. I recall being perfectly happy as a young lad, playing with friends, running up and down that corridor or in the street, making our own fun.

Surprisingly, when I was boy I used to go to the mosque in Sunel every day for prayers, and my father jokingly said: "He will become a Mullah." In fact the opposite happened to me. I did not like the madrassas, the religious schools, where we were told not to take food from non-Muslims. There was also a poem with a line that translated as "Don't eat sweets made by Hindus". Such teaching seemed to cut across everything I was learning at home, both by word and by example. Instinctively I knew it was wrong. Quite apart from anything else, if we wanted Hindus to buy sweets from us, why should we not accept sweets from them? When my father built his hospital in 1925, he put up a plaque saying: "This hospital is for all castes and creeds." Such acts almost of defiance towards the custom and habits of a nation won him many friends.

My mother, who was from Iran, joined a big population of Iranians in Mumbai (I speak Hindi, Urdu and Gujarati, but at home we speak English together). Although my mother was not formally educated, she was very far-sighted and she would mix with every community – Muslims, Hindus and other faiths – regardless of background, even in a small place like Sunel. To some she could come across as a bit fierce, fiery, even a bit of a controller, but I saw tenacity and determination, which she needed to bring up her family alone. As far as I was concerned my mother was pivotal in the formation of my character and my ethics.

My mother was a spiritual person. She was a Shia Muslim but adopted the faith of my father's Muslim Bohra sect and could speak the Bohra language, which is Gujarati, fluently. She used to read the Koran every morning until she died and I treasure the copy she used; it has pride of place in my London office beneath the bust of her that I commissioned. She was religious but not fanatical. She instilled moral values in us rather than religion, and those values have been my guide throughout my private and business life. From the beginning in Mumbai, and since I moved to the UK, I have put integrity at the top of my agenda. Businesses are built not only on skill but also on integrity; you must not cheat or short-change anyone.

Although we were not well off, in rural Sunel or Bhawani Mandi you could live a comfortable life on relatively little. We had an "open house" policy and everyone was welcome. When there was a feast day, for example, my parents would make sure we invited non-Muslims for the occasion. When I later moved on to the Fort and Proprietary High School in Mumbai, at my mother's encouragement I would always mix with a wide variety of fellow pupils, not just Muslims. So "Cosmopolitan-ness" was instilled in us and we always had non-Muslim, Christian and Jewish friends. From those earliest days we were known to be a most secular family and for that I give complete credit to my mother.

I dwell on these matters because today, as I prepare these words, it seems to me that the example my parents were demonstrating at the beginning of the last century is so applicable in the modern world. We still have religious intolerance, caste discrimination, indeed discrimination in general. A country like the United Kingdom, which is bursting at the seams with immigrants of every nationality, has to learn how to cope with them from a purely practical point of view. Everyone on this tiny island has also to find some way of getting along. The sign over my father's little hospital in Sunel spoke volumes about openness and compassion towards all people and is a lesson from which individuals today could learn.

Probably my earliest and most vivid memory as a boy is of the time when the British ship, *Fort Stikine*, exploded in Mumbai's Victoria Dock on 14 April 1944. Japanese forces were closing in on Burma and everyone assumed that this was the long-expected attack on India. It caused thousands to flee in panic from the city. The blast was so great that it split the ship in two, sunk dozens of other ships and left more than 700 people dead. The shock waves from the explosion shattered all the windows in our apartment block and for miles around.

In fact the explosion was caused by a fire on board, which broke out as the crew were about to unload a cargo of cotton bales, timber, gunpowder and ammunition – a dangerous combination! Also on board were gold bars worth £2 million at that time, which had been despatched from London to prop up the flagging Indian rupee, which was under pressure because of the war and the perceived threat from Japan. There is a story that one gold bar crashed through the roof of a Parsi gentleman called D.C. Motivala more than a mile from the docks, and he dutifully returned it. Over time the bullion was recovered but as late as the 1970s dredging operations in the harbour were still finding the occasional golden trophy in the muddy waters.[1]

What should have been a joyous time, the end of the war, was for us just the beginning of a period of anxiety and tragedy. Unexpectedly, on 18 July 1945, my elder brother (or half-brother as he would be known in the West), Mohammed Husain, died from hepatitis and typhoid. Seven months later, on 13 February 1946, my father died from the grief of losing, in effect, his eldest son. Medical bills had hit us hard leading up to this time, eating up all our savings, and once again we were reduced to living in two rooms where we slept, washed and ate. My father's prolonged illness and eventual death naturally meant that the family sweet business also suffered. Realising that we faced virtual destitution, my brother-in-law, Mohammed Husain, married to my half-sister, Fatima, had stepped in and assumed responsibility for day-to-day control of the business, and in a short time had helped restored a sense of equilibrium to our lives. He left his own business in Calcutta to help us.

As I moved into my teens I began to think of my own future and my role. I was not the oldest but I felt a strange compulsion that I had to perform for the sake of everyone else. No one expected it of me, but I wanted and welcomed the responsibility. I felt it was not a burden but a duty, just as my

---

[1] It is worth noting that the islands that once made up Bombay – or "Bom Baia", Good Bay, in Portuguese – were given to King Charles II of England as part of his dowry on his marriage to the Portuguese Princess Catharine of Braganza in 1662. Six years later the East India Company leased Bombay from the crown for just £10 per annum in gold.

father and uncle had instinctively assumed that they had a duty to build a hospital and provide accommodation for others less fortunate than themselves. The way that I was going to fulfil my duty was through the family business, but turning a local sweet shop into a multi-million-pound company was to be a tough journey.

This was just the beginning of the tumultuous life fate had in store for me – one moment great happiness, and then the next being brought down to earth with a jolt. I assume it must be the same for everyone; you either get knocked over by these events and slide into depression and sorrow, or you pick yourself up and march on. I am the type of person who is always ready to bounce back – I have had plenty of practice throughout my life, as will become apparent.

It was also an increasingly difficult time for India, which in 1946 saw riots on the streets as the clamour for Partition was whipped into a frenzy, turning once friendly neighbours into the bitterest of enemies. In 1947 the rioting became more ferocious – I would call it simply butchery. As young lads growing up in that environment, however, we just made the best of what we had. Most of the time, like any youngsters, we were oblivious of what was unfolding around us.

We played our games of cricket on the street outside our apartment, listened to test match reports from London on the radio, and there was always the cinema. My mother was a stickler for our not being out late – we had to be home by 7 p.m. – so it had to be the matinee performance, but I don't remember this as being a curb on my freedom: it was just my mother being protective. There was nothing overly cautious about the way I learned to swim. I would be dropped down a well with a rope tied round my waist, then when I had had enough I would be hauled out again – this continued until I was proficient enough to swim in the river. Eventually we would have enough money to go to a public swimming pool.

Compared with children today who are wary about even walking down the street in some places, I would say that we had tremendous freedom without temptations such as smoking or drinking to lead us astray. In short, at that age I remember being content and blissfully unaware of the turmoil that was tearing India apart.

Occasionally, however, the trouble did break into our childlike world. Every now and then there would be a rumour about some killing or other, and the tension would build up again. We must have been warned not to stray too far from home, although I do not remember feeling restricted in any way. We simply knew our boundaries and stuck to them. Muslims and Hindus kept themselves to themselves, confined to their own neighbourhoods. Fortunately my school was a five-minute walk from home in the same street and I never ventured far beyond the area. Even though Mumbai itself was the most cosmopolitan of cities, there was a ghetto mentality in those days. I am sad to say that the same mentality exists today wherever you travel in the world, even in London. In areas like Southall, which have become predominantly Asian, there are even divisions within those districts.

I was too young to understand the ramifications of Partition. When we saw the lights, we climbed on a truck to watch the flashes in the night sky. To my young eyes it must have looked like a festival – little did I realise at the time the terrible bloodshed that was taking place. The surprise is that we did not clash with our rulers of 300 years, the British Raj, and we did not turn on them. Instead we killed our own people, and that is the bitter irony of India's Independence. We gave the British a great send-off, and I am pleased with that because we can now flourish in the UK, but we killed our own kind. Partition in my view was a crime. India was a melting pot of religions. To divide the country on the basis of religion was a mistake; from today's perspective, it was a terrible mistake. The politicians should have sorted it out in a different way. Ironically, the man who championed the cause of Pakistan, Muhammad Ali Jinnah, died just seven months after Partition.

I believe most fair-minded Indian Muslims are able to absorb the culture and religions of all communities to find a way of getting along. You will always get the extremists, but our natural inclination is to be friendly and courteous. In the business world two brothers may start a family business and run it happily. It is possible that their children might get along but there is no guarantee that their cousins or future generations will see eye to eye. I have been asked to arbitrate in a number of cases like this and I always advise people that they must have a succession sorted out. If it is a big business it can be shared out; otherwise the family will fight among themselves and kill the business. The focus has to be the business.

There is a family called Ambani in India who own Reliance, India's biggest private sector company. It was founded by Dhirubhai Ambani, a brilliant man and a great entrepreneur who had started out as a petrol pump attendant. His two sons, Mukesh and Anil, had a difference of opinion – in fact their relationship became very acrimonious, and their mother had to calm them down and broker a settlement between them. But they were wise enough to divide up the operation and both are now flourishing. Mukesh Ambani is said to be one of the richest men, if not the richest man, in the world with a personal fortune running into many billions of dollars. But you cannot parcel up a country like that when so much is the same, whether it be religion or even food. India would have been the biggest, most influential country in South East Asia if it had not been for Partition.

This was a decisive moment in all our lives. Partition had just happened; my brother and father had died just months earlier. The turmoil in my mother's mind must have been unbearable. A very close family friend, Lady Nusrat Haroon – who lived in Pakistan and also hailed from Shiraz in Persia, and who was like a sister to my mother – offered to help. She suggested that if my mother wanted to close the business and move the whole family to Pakistan she would make the necessary arrangements. But my mother decided that Mumbai was where my father, uncle and brother were buried and that this was where the business was based, so somehow we would manage. In fact Lady Haroon and her family would feature again in my life and career, but at this stage my mother's renowned determination to stick it out won the day. One can only imagine what might have been had we left India behind.

While it would be misleading to suggest that politics was high on my agenda while I was still no more than a boy, other ideas were certainly beginning to take a firm hold in my mind. I distinctly remember deciding that life should be better for us and resolving to escape the impoverished conditions in which we were trapped – living cheek by jowl with our neighbours, and having to share a common toilet with everyone else on the landing. Although we just accepted the way things were and got on with it, I was conscious that there was a better life. I decided then that to have quality of life you must earn it.

A journalist once wrote that I was vulgar because I am fond of saying "There is no substitute for money". As I said at the time, he is entitled to his view; but I know what my real motivations and ambitions are and I know what was required to achieve those ambitions. When as a young boy I saw my mother and family in such dire straits, there was nothing vulgar about knowing what had to be done, if not by me then by someone else in the family, to pull us up by our bootstraps so that we could escape such hardships. Later, when I wanted my businesses to grow, there was indeed no substitute for money if I wanted to build new factories and employ more people. I had no idea how I was going to make money but I suppose I must have assumed that I would go into the family business one day.

I also had one other asset that came as a direct result of having lived in a single room – my understanding of food. The smell of the spices and the daily preparation of the modest meals were inescapable; slowly but surely I must have absorbed what I saw and what I tasted. I never wrote recipes down and I don't recall asking what my mother was putting into the dishes, but somehow or other I learned the basic building blocks of my future in that room, in the smoke and clatter of pots and pans and the joyful chaos of family mealtimes. Because my mother could not afford to do anything else, she prepared simple meals in the traditional way with natural ingredients. It is that authenticity that I have fought to preserve in the dishes we prepare in their millions today.

Later, as I built my business, I would always insist that meals should be cooked using the recipes – even the methodology, albeit with modern conveniences – of the housewives at home in India. I was never prepared to compromise on these essential requirements even though I came close to losing what was to become my best client as a result of my stubbornness. Quality of ingredients, quality of preparation, indeed quality in all things, was a standard I inherited from my mother. There could be no compromise. In the food business there is often a temptation to succumb to the use of inferior raw material just to swell your bottom line, but I would never do that. We never diluted the quality of our meals, and I am constantly searching for the best of the best ingredients for my products as I am in my life.

An early family photograph, from l to r: my father, brother Abbas, brother Mohammed Hussain, sister Ateka, my mother with Akbar as a baby. In front I am standing with my nephew Kamru (right).

Aged six, with my father.

With my daughters, Zeenat and Zarmin.

Family group with my mother. Back row, l to r: Mohammad Hussain, Lady Nusrat Haroun, my mother, a friend, Fattuben. In front: GN, my nephew Kamru and Laila Sarfraz.

Public hospital built by my father and uncle in Sunel, 1928.

Royal Sweets shop Mumbai (circa 1957) where I began my career.

From an early age hunting became a passion.

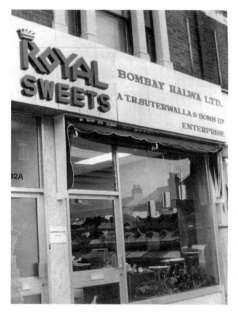

Royal Sweets' first shop in London, circa 1972

With childhood friend, Syed Ahmed Hussain.

Famous Indian artist, M. F. Husain, holds a portrait he painted of my brother in 1936.

Railway station of Bhawani Mandi. l to r: Ibrahim and Abdullah, Mohini and her mother Amrit

At the inauguration of accommodation for local police at Sunel – built by me!

With His Highness Prince Agha Khan. Shehzada Qaid Zohar Bhai Saheb is in the background.

With actress Susan Hampshire. She launched the Noon brand (1992).

In 1994 a devastating fire destroyed Noon Products.

Opening of Noon Products in 1995, with Yum Yum Club members. Mrs Laxmi Shirdasami, Chairman of Yum Yum is to my right.

With Lord Sainsbury and Lord Ashdown when I became 'Asian of the Year'.

Receiving 'Asian of the Year' award in 1994 from Rt. Hon. Michael Heseltine, Deputy Prime Minister.

At a House of Commons reception to celebrate my knighthood. From l to r: Shaikh Shabbir Abidali, Zherada Amar Bhai Saheb Jamaluddin, Mohini, GN, Shehzada Qaid Zohar Bhai Saheb and Dr Zainuddin.

With HRH Prince Charles at the opening of a new factory of Noon Products in 203.

Chapter Three

THE START OF NOON THE BUSINESSMAN

Although I left school at the age of seventeen with not much more than a few basic qualifications, I did make two significant decisions. I would throw myself wholeheartedly into the family business and I would throw away the name "Gulam"! I hated it, and decided to adopt the nickname my mother had given me, "Noon". To be honest I have no idea why I was called that, but it stuck. Everyone now calls me Noon, although the British still find it a little difficult – perhaps because it suggests too much familiarity – and, despite my protestations, some insist on saying "Sir Gulam", or in certain sections of society "GK". But I am happy with just plain "Noon".

As for my career path, I always knew that commerce was the right direction for me. In fact before I left school, I started my own business called Commercial Arts and Printers when I was just sixteen, taking on small printing jobs. But that was only a schoolboy distraction before I could get stuck in to the real thing.

The family business, "Kamruddin Ebrahamjee", was run out of two small shops opposite Mumbai's Crawford Market, a vast 72,000 square foot, sprawling indoor site situated on a busy junction near the Victoria Terminus railway station. It was named after Sir Arthur Crawford, the city's first Municipal Commissioner, and was the first building in India to be lit by electricity. It epitomised Victorian India and is still on the tourist trail. Visitors can admire design of a bygone age, including panelling on the exterior said to be the work of John Lockwood Kipling, Mumbai's Municipal Architect at the time and the father of Rudyard Kipling, the author of such favourites as *The Jungle Book*, *Just So Stories*, "If" and many more. (Rudyard was born in Mumbai and died six days before I was born.)

We opened early like all the other shops and stalls in the market to escape the worst of the day's heat. The sweets were displayed in glass cabinets or in ready packs, and from that point of view nothing much has changed. Every day after school I would spend time in the shops and was given minor tasks like cleaning and polishing the furniture. In all Indian businesses everyone contributes in some way, old and young alike knowing that in the end everyone benefits. Eventually I graduated to working on the till and was allowed to meet the customers.

My company accountant, who had worked with my father and his brother previously, thought that he saw some business potential in me – perhaps because I was always asking questions – and arranged for me to visit a teacher to learn the basic principles of accountancy. Later he insisted that I should write up the books at the end of each day. This taught me the most essential requirement of any business: always know exactly what is in your accounts.

My business genes may have come from my father's being a shopkeeper, but from my mother there came a different wisdom: she used to say, "You will be known by the friends you keep." I was a quick learner and always had educated friends – and even today I am ready to learn from anyone. I was determined to improve my lot, and when I left school I arranged to have lessons to improve not only my accountancy but also my English. I learned from India's first Prime Minister, Jawaharlal Nehru: when he introduced his first five-year plan for the economy in 1951, a system that continues to this day, I decided that our business should have one too. I was only fifteen at the time and I must have been a fairly precocious teenager as the business was still being run by my brother-in-law, Mohammed Husain.

Gradually, while I was still in my early twenties, I effectively took control of the business and began making changes. My brother-in-law had done a good job and had been there when we needed him most. In effect, when we inherited the business from my father and checked the books we realised it was virtually bankrupt, so my brother-in-law had put the business back on its feet. He did a first-class job and can honestly be said to have saved the business and the family from certain ruin. He was essentially a shopkeeper but he had a great influence on my approach to business life. I would not want to belittle his skills, because if he had not taught me the basics I could never have become an industrialist.

The sweet business was a training in the essentials of manufacturing: you buy sugar and you buy oil and the various ingredients, then you manufacture your product, work out your costs and the rest is profit. All manufacturing is the same. While my brother-in-law always supported me as I moved the business forward, he did not have vision in the business sense of the word; he was not able to train me in how to become an entrepreneur. I knew I had to do something radical if I was going to be able to support the family.

Although we came from the same background I was already different. My friends were more cosmopolitan: they were Jews, Christians, Sikhs and Hindus as well as Muslims. Above all I had the quest, the thirst and the capacity to learn and to improve myself. I was having the extra accountancy and English lessons, as I have mentioned. As a teenager I had started writing to a girl in Australia as a pen-friend to improve my English – I still remember her name, Hazel Hutchinson. Even today, because I have to give a lot of speeches I have lessons in how to improve my oratory – you can never stop learning. In fact, I went to learn public speaking skills at Lord Janner's school of oratory in London.

While Indians like to have their sweets displayed in the traditional way, I was determined that the business should not be held back by old-fashioned practices. The first thing to do was to install air conditioning and smarten up the shop with better-quality furniture and fittings. I even hired an architect to redesign the layout. Everyone – friends as well as business rivals – said I was making the shops look too grand and too expensive, like jewellery shops, and warned me that no one would come in because they did not look like sweet shops. In fact customer numbers increased immediately – they welcomed if nothing else the opportunity to escape from the heat outside.

I am not a traditionalist, and I do not copy something just because my next-door neighbour has it; I like to go one step beyond that. I am a stickler for traditional ingredients but I was always ready to use new techniques to prepare the food. People like to copy because it is the easier option; I like to do something different in order to be ahead of the crowd. If you want to add value to your business, you have to come up with new ideas and be creative. Even at home I design my own furniture or I get someone in to design it according to my idea because I don't like to have the same thing as everyone else. Most people buy their Christmas cards but I come up with my own individual card every year

I also had to push through a more drastic change and the family took some convincing. The name "Kamruddin Ebrahamjee" on the fascia was obviously Muslim, and I decided it was simply putting off non-Muslims from coming into the shops. At Diwali, when we should have been at our busiest, we were twiddling our thumbs. I had to change the name. My mother, who was still alive, was furious and slapped my face for what she perceived to be an insult to my uncle's memory. Of course nothing could have been further from the truth and, despite the short-term upset I insisted on changing the name to "Royal Sweets". First and foremost the name had no religious connotations, and it struck me that the "regal" tone would be appreciated by our customers. Indians like the best and the finest and no one seemed to be concerned about associations between royalty and the Empire. As with the air conditioning, the positive impact on our turnover was immediate.

Perhaps it is worth noting here that this was the first time that my mother had slapped me. The second occasion was to teach me a lesson in humiliation. My mother had always taught us that to be a good Muslim you had to respect all people, regardless of faith or race. Some years later when I was a grown man, married with a child, and I heard that we had landed a big contract, I shouted, "I've done it." Her stinging slap landed on my cheek. I was stunned and asked her why she had done that. "You did not do it alone," was her rebuke. I have never forgotten her words.

With her new independence, India was now looking beyond her borders as she planned her future growth. While there had to be an internal structure and strategy for the country, it was clear that India had to look abroad for help. The result today is that India is courted by all sides because of her economic strength and the strategic importance of her geographical position. It would not be too much of an exaggeration to say that I had similar thoughts about Royal Sweets in that I knew we could not hope to change our lives for the better if we continued with only two shops. We had to be bold and expand, otherwise we would continue in nothing more than a hand-to-mouth existence. I knew there was no choice, and for once I was happy to follow the example of others. Many of my school friends and neighbours and even some of my family members had decided to look abroad for prosperity, and all eyes were turned either to America or to England.

To describe our lives as "a hand-to-mouth existence" may be putting things a bit strongly. We were employing an increasing number of people including members of the family, and our sales had increased considerably in just a few short years. The business was, of course, dedicated to my father's memory and name. Nevertheless I felt limited, even restricted, by our business model. Not only that, but I was becoming fascinated by all things technological – I would enjoy films like Steven Spielberg's *Jurassic Park* in future years simply because of the ingenious special effects. The special effect I realised we needed at Royal Sweets was an injection of modern technology. If the business was to take off, we could not rely on a few people in the backroom making sweets, like a cottage industry. We had to expand production, and that meant modernisation and a degree of automation.

I should explain a little how the sweets were prepared and, to a large extent, how they still are prepared in many shops throughout the world. These are not sweets as westerners might understand them. They are often served at the end of a meal as a dessert and also, as I have mentioned, they are handed round on important occasions. The basic ingredients are sugar, milk, fat and flour. There are probably hundreds of different varieties, and each region of India has its own speciality, but they may be broadly divided into two categories – milk-based and flour-based sweets. Many sweets also contain "khoa" or "mava", which is milk boiled to remove all the moisture.

Let me digress here to tell a story about the VAT man in the UK. Indian sweets are considered to be part of a meal. They are not luxuries but part and parcel of Indian life – some people eat "sweets" only at meal times. They are traditionally part of religious ceremonies, other festivals and every significant event in human life. I had a long correspondence with the VAT commissioners in the early 1970s before I was formally able to establish this distinction and VAT was removed from Indian sweets.

When I started out, sweet-making was indeed still very much a cottage industry. Take just one sweet, a burfi, as an example: this is a typical Indian fudge made out of concentrated milk, with sugar and nuts and some flavouring, and would be put together by housewives, slowly and laboriously. Hardly cost-effective! This work was all done on site in the backrooms of shops.

The answer was to prepare the sweets off site in a factory, because manufacturing and sales had to be separated. We used special jacketed steam vessels with temperature controls. As a result we were now making thousands of varieties of sweets instead of only a limited range and small volumes. This was a radical step and I had to persuade my brother-in-law, as head of the family, that buying a 5000 square foot factory was a wise decision. The business grew faster and more shops were opened in Bandra, Andheri and Grant Road in Mumbai. Today all our sweets are made at the factory in Sewri. Although the word "factory" sounds a bit industrial, what emerges from the process is mouth-watering enough to ensure that we have a loyal client base of individuals and corporations. We make every variety of sweet, including raspberry and rose halwas, kaju and kesar katlis; some cakes are sweetened with honey, and others with dates and figs. In short, we offer a vast selection with literally something for everyone.

I wouldn't want to give the impression that all this progress and modernisation was entirely thanks to me. Throughout my life I have followed my mother's advice and learnt from others, and one of my earliest influences was my brother-in-law, Mohammed Husain. So often in life you can have a great idea but not have the backing of someone who can turn your dreams into reality. I was lucky but I was also blessed with a capacity for hard work: after all, I had been prepared to spend my childhood years at the shop. In young adulthood, I would arrive early and leave late at around

8.30 p.m. I had a bed on a mezzanine floor at the shop and I would cat-nap for a couple of hours during the heat of the midday sun before getting on with some more work late into the evening. You might say the entrepreneurship was beginning to surface. I must have always had an innate business sense: nature plays its part; it is either in you or it is not. It is in the psyche.

Chapter Four

THE VELVET COUP AND DREAMS OF LONDON

Not everyone fulfils or even finds their his or her dreams but we all have them, inspired by people we meet, books we read or images we see. Books did not play a big part in my early life, and I opted to go to work rather than try for a university place and a degree. However, I am inordinately proud today to have been awarded five honorary doctorate degrees by British universities. At one of the ceremonies, when I received the degree of Master of the University of Surrey, I told the young students wearing their black gowns and caps: "It has taken you three years to get your degrees but it has taken me forty years."

For me the dreams were first conjured up on the flickering screen of my local cinema. Remember that we had no television, and no other "canned" entertainment as young people do today beyond the crackly radio. There was no drink, no drugs, no womanising, but we did have the cinema every Sunday, and it was cheap – costing the equivalent of about 10p. I was transfixed by the Arthur Rank movies and in particular by the newsreels from London with pictures of the Changing of the Guard at Buckingham Palace, Piccadilly Circus and Madame Tussaud's. This is where I got my inspiration, my wanderlust if you like, and for me there was only one place to go. Other friends had decided on America but I knew that my first destination once out of India would have to be England; and not just England, but London.

As soon as I could, I promised myself, I would get a passport. Then I would work out how I was going to get to England and, once there, how I would survive. I wrote to a former classmate who was already in London and he assured me that I could get a job at £9 per week, and to start with I would be able to live with him to keep my costs down. I wish I had kept his letter.

I was determined to travel by ship. Everything was perfectly clear in my young mind. Then one day the opportunity arose. I booked my ticket on P&O's liner *Strathmore* and only then broke the news to my mother. She was devastated and implored me not to go. Having been widowed twice by the time she was just forty, and having already lost one son at a young age, it was in her eyes as if she was now about to lose another son forever. She assumed that once I had left for England I would never return. I could see her grief, and although I am sure that I tried to explain to her that it was only a visit, it must have been obvious to me that she could not understand, so I succumbed to the emotional pressure and called the whole thing off.

All my energies were now focused on developing the business, with the clear aim of improving our standard of living. If I had to give up my plans of travelling to England, I could at least aspire to some of the good life I saw there. I replaced my bicycle, which I had bought from my first salary cheque of 100 rupees, with a motorbike, and later with my first car, a Morris Minor convertible!

Once again I upset tradition by moving into a separate apartment of my own after I got married to Raeka in 1960. Traditionally, Indian sons bring their brides to live in the family home, but I wanted my independence. My mother and various other members of the family were all living in the same block of flats. We were now in larger apartments with three bedrooms, a kitchen and a large hall, but it must have felt claustrophobic to me with so many members of the family living on top of one another and I decided to move out. Not only had I started showing signs of entrepreneurial independence but I now wanted some form of personal independence, some freedom as I started my own family.

This was also the start of my business interests away from food because I thought there was an opportunity to make money in property. Our main shop was in an apartment block that I decided could be profitable if it were managed properly. The owner himself tried to put me off, warning me that all the rent went on maintenance costs. But I persisted and we agreed a price. The owner said I was a brave young man and wished me luck. I was twenty-five years old. Of course, I was committing the family to a major leap of faith, but I went ahead with the deal and only then set about convincing my family that it was a good idea. I remember waiting until my mother and my brother-in-law were together before telling them what I had done. Mohammed Husain was horrified and said to my mother, "You see – I told you he would make us all bankrupt one day." My mother looked at me and said I should have spoken to my brother-in-law about it first. I said that if I had done that he would not have agreed to the deal. I could tell that secretly my mother was impressed and proud of my enterprise.

That was another turning point in our fortunes. It was probably also the moment at which everyone accepted that, when it came to business matters, I would take the decisions even though I was not the oldest. It was a defining moment in my business career: a coming of age. There was no formal board meeting to make me "chairman", nor any announcement. My takeover just emerged. It may be instructive for budding entrepreneurs to see how that came about. My brother-in-law must have been bemused by the volume of business we were now doing and he started to become indecisive. My principle has always been that power is never given, it is snatched – even if it is from your father – and I still believe that philosophy today. So to a great extent I snatched control of the business, albeit in a gradual way. Naturally Mohammed Husain was not pleased at first, pointing out quite rightly that when I was a mere stripling he had rescued the business and now here I was trying to take over. But slowly I explained to him how things could be improved.

There were some classic examples. When business was flourishing he had a great habit of delaying payments to his suppliers. The supplier would come on a Saturday and he would say no, come back on Wednesday. I would watch this performance, but what could I do? I could not override him. He was only doing it to show some sort of power over them. But basic diplomacy was involved. So once when he was on holiday I told the accountant that in future we would send a card out to our suppliers telling them when they should come and collect their cheques and that the accounts department would take care of the whole transaction. When my brother-in-law returned he commented after a few weeks that no one was coming to collect their money, so I explained that I did not want the suppliers troubling him. He was an established businessman – he should not be bothering with mere suppliers. Diplomacy again, but he could not fault the new arrangements.

Take another example. Mohammed Husain kept two leather pouches in his desk – one for income tax and one for sales tax. Every day he would mentally calculate what we owed and put say 500 rupees or 5000 rupees into the appropriate pouch. I watched this for a while and eventually said it was too dangerous to keep so much money on the premises. It had been all right when it was a small business, but now we were dealing with much larger sums. I recommended that we should open a separate bank account to hold the money – surely we were business-like enough not to spend it. In other words, the "velvet coup" to take over control had already begun.

Then I started advertising, which he did not believe in, and the name over the shop was changed, which upset everyone including my mother, as I have said – although to this day the business is registered under my uncle's name. But I had the courage of my own convictions, and if I hadn't "snatched the power" we would not be where we are today. My brother-in-law still came in every day and was shown every respect and courtesy, as was his due, and he gave his formal approval to everything with a nod of the head. It took a while for this benign, constitutional monarchy style of business to be established. Nothing was said, but he knew that the reins of power were now in my hands. He was still King, but he could not refuse me, his Prime Minister.

Initially everything that I suggested should be done he opposed. When I bought the car for my mother he said no, when I bought my car he said no, when I wanted to move the manufacturing he said no, and when I even bought his apartment for him he said no. So in the end I just took the decisions and announced that I had done so afterwards. Later he accepted that it was the wise thing to do. My brother-in-law was an honest and caring man who encouraged and taught me so much about the basics of business.

He was sensible enough to recognise the changing times, and he soon accepted my business acumen and was able to let go.

It would be foolish to claim that everything was sweetness and light, however. There was some friction between other members of the extended family, some of whom thought they had rights to the business through accident of marriage, and there was jealousy from the more remote relatives when they saw me taking over. Although my mother was anxious not to confront them, I did not hesitate to protect what had been my "sweat equity" invested throughout my early childhood and as a young man. I had put in the time and taken the risks despite opposition and now the family was benefiting. Yes, I was in a powerful position and I suppose there was a certain amount of youthful arrogance, but I had worked hard and was successful. It came to a nasty exchange of lawyers' letters at one point but I warned them that I had never lost in litigation and I was not prepared to start losing now. The action was dropped. It was accepted that I now had full authority in the family business.

It is no good just having an idea and not implementing it or not being prepared to work hard. But I was blessed with all the ingredients: I had been born with a business brain, I was physically fit, I was prepared to put in long hours and I was a risk taker. Not only did I have all those benefits, but I also had good friends.

Being fit probably helped me, maybe even saved my life, in 1968. I was flying back to India with a friend, and being Shia Muslims we decided we would stop over to pay our respects at the tomb of our Prophet's grandson when we reached Baghdad. A couple of days later we took an Iraqi Airways flight to Kuwait. It was a Viscount aeroplane with four propellers. We took off with twenty-six passengers plus crew on board. About ten minutes into the flight I noticed an oil slick on my window. Moments later the pilot came out of his cockpit to check because obviously he had seen warning lights on his instrument panel.

He immediately announced that we would be returning to Baghdad because of a technical snag. He took us over a desert and we began circling as he dumped fuel – a standard precaution, as it was dangerous to land with a full load of aviation fuel. As we came in to land we were all asked to assume the brace position. It was a tense few moments. As I felt the main undercarriage hit the ground I breathed a sigh of relief, but as the nose wheel came down it broke. What I had seen on my window was the hydraulic fuel from the front wheel. The aircraft went out of control and we thought that at any moment it would topple over. The cabin filled with smoke. We veered off the runway into a ploughed field, which fortunately acted as a brake, and we stopped. We could see the Iraqi fire brigade following us but they did not come any closer because they were afraid of an explosion.

The young pilot came out and he and I struggled to open the door, but the alignment was haywire because of the crash landing. It seemed like a long time but was probably only a minute or so, and between us we forced the door open and started pushing people out onto the wing. From there they jumped down, which was a bit like jumping from a first-floor window – there was of course no emergency chute to slide down on the old Viscounts. Finally the Iraqi emergency services approached and started taking off the children and ladies. The plane was now on fire and there was clearly a risk of explosion.

My friend, who was a little heavy, jumped and broke his leg. I jumped down after him and ran to see what I could do. There was some internal bleeding and so he was rushed to hospital. Fortunately we both happened to have our passports in our pockets so I arranged for him to be sent him back to Mumbai the next day by Kuwait airways on a stretcher and I went on to Kuwait. All our luggage went up in flames and the aircraft was totally destroyed. I am sure that if the pilot and I had not been strong enough to open the door there might have been someone else who would have done so, but it does not do to dwell on the alternatives! It was a shocking experience and for a couple of years I felt uncomfortable about flying. For some time I would certainly opt for the train when travelling inside India.

Throughout most of my twenties I was fixated on the business, but I also instinctively understood that I could not stay selling sweets forever. I found myself waking up thinking of sweets, playing cricket thinking of sweets and going to bed thinking of sweets. Although I only worked it out much later in my thirties, I can now explain to young businessmen and businesswomen that if you spend your whole life thinking about your business and fine-tuning it you are wearing blinkers and you will always remain in that one place. That's why chefs are so good at what they do – they are always refining their recipes; but they remain chefs all their lives.

I wanted to diversify. I was already interested in property, but in 1969 I started my Paper Print and Product Company to supply various paper brands, and I launched the Noon Blister Packs Company, which produces sealed packs for items such as toothbrushes and plastic trays for sweets. These companies are both still running profitably today.

There is another important point here about decision-making. Perhaps it was a result of the hesitancy or negativity that I encountered, but I soon realised that I always wanted to be in a position where I could make up my own mind and take a decision to act. You can surround yourself with advisers and consultants, but I always ask myself why, if the management consultant is so good at running my sort of business, he is not doing so himself. It is good to take advice and to be prepared to learn, but in the end you make your own decision, and that's the way I have run my life. There are people who cannot work without consulting each other. I will consult everybody, but in the end I will do exactly what I want to do. I am just as happy to take the criticism when things go wrong, as they occasionally do, as to take the rewards.

To that extent I have become a loner. I am at my best when I don't have to ask people. That's my temperament. Royal Sweets in India I built by taking critical decisions without seeking advice. Paper Print I built alone. Noon Blister I built alone. I know my own strength. If I have to ask people they waver, and then they upset my mindset. When I was renovating the sweet shop they asked if I was starting a jewellery shop, but I carried on and finished the job. Then when I decided to shift my factory from the shop to a site a few miles away they said I was defeating the object of having my manufacturing base close by, but I went ahead. When I started the Paper Print business they asked me what I knew about the industry. I would never have done anything if I had listened to the advice I received from all and sundry. When the time came to move to London, I knew that my success or failure would depend on me.

It is important to point out that all my life I have been fortunate in being blessed with a tremendous team – management and staff. In Bombay I was confident enough to leave my managing director, Arif Bandukwalla, in charge. He was the son of a late, dear friend, Firoz Bandukwalla. He joined me straight from graduation and today still manages both Paper and Print, and Blister Pack.

I understood very early on that I wanted to be in control of my own destiny. If you are a risk taker, as I am, people may become afraid and your partners may be worried. But if you are convinced about a course of action or a deal, you should go for it without hesitation. Those who are cautious may also have their reasons, but when I am the only one to blame it is my skin, my neck on the chopping block. When I am alone I am confident about my decisions. Similarly when I became a non-executive director of companies in later life I was not afraid to speak my mind and tell the truth regardless of whether I was working with ministers or with official bodies. I remember when I was at a meeting of the TFL, the London transport body, I asked why the American Embassy staff were getting away with not paying the congestion charge when smaller, less affluent embassies were doing so. I told the Mayor of London, Ken Livingstone, that I hoped he was not just going to write it off in the books. It would have been easier for me not to rock the boat.

Although I may have run my businesses as a loner, in my personal life I now had a young family to care for. My daughter, Zeenat, was born in 1961. Life for all the family prospered. Indeed life in India prospered: the population increased by more than 20 per cent between 1951 and 1961, and it would have been simple for me just to carry on with a quiet and steady life. But that's not my style.

Chapter Five

‿∾⊶⊶⋙⊱⊰⋘⊷⊷∾‿

Bringing Royal Sweets to England

The lure of the UK was too strong, and one June day in 1966 I told my mother that I wanted to go and visit – just for a holiday, but I needed to get it out of my system. Either there would be an opportunity for me or there wouldn't, but I had to see for myself. This time she agreed. I suppose she must have realised that there was no point refusing. The family was now settled so she probably also felt more secure.

Yusuf Haroon, a distinguished political figure from Pakistan who had also been encouraging me to visit, offered to pay for my ticket – £178 on Kuwaiti Airways, which I would later repay. Our two families were close and I had always considered his mother as my aunt and her children as cousins. My mother had immense respect for him, and as children we always thought that his mother, Lady Nusrat Haroon,[1] and my mother were sisters. Much later we found that while they were both from Shiraz and were old friends, they were not even distant relatives.

And so a month later on 30 July, with a few pounds in my pocket, I flew into Heathrow. It was love at first sight. I went to an hotel that Mr Haroon had booked for me in Victoria – the Oxford House Hotel, £1 per day with

---

[1] Lady Haroon was the wife of Sir Abdullah Haroon, a successful sugar magnate who was a key figure at the time of Partition, guiding the Partition of India resolution in the Sindh Provincial Muslim League Conference in October 1938. He was later knighted by the British.

breakfast. He lived in a stylish apartment in Park Lane. After a nap to recover from the overnight flight, I took a bus straight to Piccadilly Circus, the sight I had seen so many times at the movies. Everyone, young and old, was drinking beer and dancing and merry-making. I stopped someone and asked what was going on. Was there a festival or something? He said no, but England had just won the World Cup against Germany.

If England was in a good mood, I was enraptured by the people and the culture. Everything about England impressed me. I remember going into a shop one day and leaving without picking up my change. A few days later when I went back the shopkeeper handed me the change that I had forgotten. I was amazed. I wonder if such a thing would happen today, but it did make a big impression on me.

I also made contact with Taherbhai Suterwalla, a neighbour of mine in India who had already developed a major grocery wholesale business in ethnic foods in London. Today it is run by his sons and is worth millions. I had found Mr Suterwalla an apartment on the floor above me in our block of flats in Mumbai. Whenever he was in India I used to go up to his apartment and have coffee with him and his family every morning before work. Some family members still recall my eccentric habit of appearing with my tie slung casually around my neck. I would later knot it before reaching the shop. Maybe he saw something in me, but he also must have realised from his own experience that if I really wanted to make my fortune it would have to be outside India, and he said that if ever I decided to open a business in the UK he would back me financially.

This was another defining moment, a key moment in my life. He was putting me to the test. Could the young upstart from India really become an international player? But it was an inauspicious start. I caught flu the moment I arrived in London – the English weather had found another easy victim. Mrs Suterwalla put me straight to bed with some tablets. When I recovered we agreed that Taherbhai Suterwalla would give me financial backing to start Royal Sweets in UK. I may be a risk taker but they are always calculated risks, so I suggested that I would begin slowly by sending him some of the perishable sweet products that his company would distribute in the UK by air and ship the non-perishables. With the arrangement agreed I returned to India. My mind was already made up: one day I would have to move my base of operations to London. Throughout the flight home I began formulating my plans, my future.

Sadly, by the time I returned to the UK Taherbhai Suterwalla had died, but his sons, Fakhruddin and Hatim, along with three younger brothers, Shiraj, Mansour and Iqbal, agreed to stand by their father's promise. We reached a commercial decision. I said I was a technocrat and I would put in my expertise and effort, and they agreed to invest the funds. Strict Indian Foreign Exchange controls meant I could not use any of my own money from India, and therefore I had to borrow. I also had to get special permission from the Indian Finance Ministry to organise a joint venture and brought seven chefs over from Mumbai on UK work permits. I felt I was beginning to make progress when I eventually bought my own house in Ruislip.

The Suterwallas and I were 50:50 partners and we floated a company called Bombay Halwa Limited with a brand name of Royal Sweets. Companies House had not allowed us to register the name Royal Sweets Limited, no doubt because of the word "Royal", which is rightly zealously protected in the UK. We opened our first shop in Broadway, Southall, in West London on 9 February 1974, having established a small factory the previous year. In the first year we set up nine franchised shops in London, Leicester and Bradford. My idea was to put a manager in to run the UK business when I was in India – I would soon find myself commuting back and forth every four months or so.

That is how the business was conceived. It was built on friendship and grew simply by word of mouth because the quality was good. There had been no specific plan as Taherbhai Suterwalla and I sat drinking those coffees back in India. As far as I was concerned he was family. He no doubt indulged me as I talked about my dreams and ambitions; perhaps he remembered his younger days when he was planning his future. He had followed his own dreams and ambitions, taken himself away from the "comfort zone" of his mother country and succeeded.

My brother-in-law, who was still alive at the time and was head of Royal Sweets in India, was worried. What if the UK business did not take off? Who was going to bear the losses? I said we were, but that was too much of a risk for him. He said he could not afford it, so we agreed that I would buy his share in the London venture. After that I never looked back. It may have been a tentative start, but I could see the great potential in the country even though many well-meaning friends urged me to think again. One of my friends came over and found me living in a small room, sharing a toilet and bathroom with the landlady. He asked why I was living like that and putting up with those conditions.

When I left India I was a Justice of the Peace appointed by the Maharashtra state government and president of the Welfare Organisation for Road Safety Patrol, India's equivalent of RoSPA (the Royal Society for the Prevention of Accidents) – my Deputy President was the Commissioner of Police, so it was quite some position. I had been the Secretary of the Sweet Meat Merchants' Association for seven years. Other members were much older than me but they really respected me. The classic example was that when we went to Delhi, the seat of the Federal government, I would go by air and stay in a five-star hotel while they would go by train and stay in an inn. But they would allow me these luxuries. I remember it came up at a meeting and the President simply said: "He is worth it." I had a good commercial life; I was friendly with senior politicians – in short I had built a good position. I had a nice apartment and chauffeur-driven car, so to ask why I had given up all those perks was indeed a fair question.

Quite simply, I was not comfortable in my "comfort zone". I needed a bigger platform, but I knew my old friends would never understand. You cannot explain that sort of drive, the restlessness that pushes you on to new challenges. You either have it or you don't. Some people are more than happy with the lives they have got and are content to "settle down". They are lucky, but I will never be able to do that. I am constantly on the lookout for new ventures, new properties and new opportunities. I don't believe it is greed or naked ambition; it is just the way I am. When I was a child staring at my father's body and seeing my mother in tears, I vowed to put things right. In the late sixties and early seventies I had another spur, the fear of failure. When you travel 5000 miles you have no option but to succeed because if you don't your ego is very badly damaged when you go back. "I told you so," people will say. I was determined never to hear those words.

There is something rather solitary, even possibly lonely, about this approach but it is the one to which I am best suited. There are people who need support and people who stand alone. I am not a true loner, but in the end I back my own hunches. That is not to say that every business I started made money. I did lose occasionally, but if out of ten businesses you create seven or eight are successful, you learn from your mistakes. I was to lose in America. I lost a lot of money in the travel agency business – but that is not to say that I would not take on a travel agency business again if the right deal came along!

Frankly, the sweet business could have gone either way. When I added up our first week's takings at the Southall shop – all of £68 – my heart sank, but I persevered. In the early days we just about broke even. My brother-in-law had not been wrong to be cautious and to step aside because he felt the risks outweighed the potential benefits. That is the sort of judgement businessmen and businesswomen make every day; sometimes they are proved right, sometimes wrong. On this occasion I got lucky.

An unlikely ally came to my rescue: "His Excellency President for Life, Field Marshal Alhaji Dr Idi Amin Dada, VC, DSO, MC, CBE", the brutal and insane dictator of Uganda. One morning he apparently woke up and said he had had a dream, the effect of which was that 35,000 Asians were expelled from the country in just three months between August and November 1972 and most of them came to England. It was an absolute tragedy for those poor people who had to leave in the clothes they stood up in, abandoning their careers and their homes, but it transformed my business and I am pleased to say, in time, it transformed many of those unfortunate people's lives for the better as well. Gradually, with their instinctive ingenuity and capacity for hard work, these refugees built new careers and many made their fortunes, rising to some of the most distinguished positions in the land. Asians make up about 5 per cent of the British population but they own more than 20 per cent of London's private businesses, and the richest man in the UK is Indian. As they all prospered, so too did Royal Sweets.

I knew by now that I would have to live full-time in the UK. The whole family was provided for, so I began my international commute.

Even after Idi Amin's intervention there was no guarantee that the business would succeed, but once again I took the risk and it paid off. Before long we had opened nine shops. The lesson here for the new entrepreneur is that if you are convinced about an idea, money is never a problem. If you have the right mental attitude and you feel capable of handling the task you set yourself, money will come –but you must put your ideas down paper and go after the money.

The Suterwallas (their brand name is TRS in business) and I had a very good partnership that was to last thirty years before I eventually offered to buy the company back. We were friends, but I realised that their method of working, while highly successful, was different from mine. We both had strong personalities, and rather than fall out we agreed that we would set a fair commercial valuation on the business and I would buy them out. The point was that while we might get along, our children might not. Also I wanted to expand the business in my own way. I knew that Bombay Halwa Limited would not go anywhere unless the whole thing was in my hands and I could run it myself. I suggested value A, they suggested value B and so I paid them value B. We parted on good terms and are still firm friends.

I had learned from a very young age that just when you think everything is going well life bowls you what in cricketing parlance is called a googly, and in 1978 my Bombay Halwa factory was destroyed by fire. The whole factory burned down. Everything was lost and we had to start again from scratch. Fire seems to have been my enemy because I had to confront it again later in London.

The business was doing reasonably well; we were not complacent but we were on our way. I was asleep at home when my general manager and director, Shabbir Kanchwala, a loyal and hardworking man who had been with me in India, called to say there was a fire. He was in tears. I rushed to the factory – it was about one o'clock in the morning. The fire had started on the first floor, which had collapsed destroying all the machinery. I tried to calm everyone down. I like to think I was fairly philosophical about it and I said it was just one of those things.

Our retail business did not suffer because I was making sweets at a laboratory level in Wokingham where I had a room with some machinery for demonstration purposes and testing out new ideas. So I started a small production line there. I also started making sweets at the back of my shop at 92 Broadway. It wasn't easy but we managed, and crucially, as far as the customers were concerned, it was business as usual. I even made sweets at the premises of one of my suppliers of raw materials in Harrow. I would go there with my chefs and make the sweets on site at night. That is how we survived. We would then load up the vans and distribute the sweets. It was a great challenge, but a useful experience because another much bigger fire would follow years later.

These sorts of adversities bring opportunity and strength. I went to Canada and bought some more steam kettles and other machinery and began rebuilding. There was nothing else to be done. We rebuilt the factory in about eight months and resumed our normal production. Things happen: it is how you react that is important. I have literally buried a lot of people in my life – friends and relatives – sometimes personally getting down in the hole and digging the earth: that is real sorrow and loss. This time no one had been killed. It was not the end of the world: it was just business. We simply had to start again.

So that's how I took it. I did not take a defeatist attitude then and I would never do so now. That sort of philosophy helped me again in 1994, when I suffered a much greater loss and my entire Noon Products business went up in flames. People thought I would go bankrupt and have to go back to India. Not me. I would rebuild. Thanks to Idi Amin, the business had been established. In 1978 Bombay Halwa stumbled momentarily, but then it grew and grew.

Now my base of operations was firmly in the UK and I had my own young family living with me. Unfortunately, on the personal side things did not work out at the time. My wife, Raeka, never really liked the UK and could not take the cold. She wanted to go back to India. I was young, perhaps a bit stubborn, so it was not entirely her fault, and in the end we agreed to part. By now we had a second daughter, Zarmin, who was born in 1969, and the decision was taken that Raeka and Zarmin would return to India and Zeenat would stay in London with me to continue her education. Later Zarmin returned to attend a boarding school in Hastings, Sussex. Raeka and I still have an amicable relationship for the sake of our daughters.

I looked after her, and she visits the UK from time to time when she stays with one of our daughters. It was a civilised parting of the ways. I always believe that instead of crying every day you should cry only once and take a decision. The same applies in business. Instead of bickering every day with your commercial partner, it is better to separate.

By the late seventies Royal Sweets was secure in both India and the UK and I could see the business set fair for steady growth. The Asian community in the UK was growing faster than ever as more and more people saw this as a land of opportunity. Just as my fellow countrymen and countrywomen were flocking to the British Isles, I was tempted by something new in a different land.

Chapter Six

American Odyssey

In the late 1970s, my good friend Yusuf Haroon invited me to the opening of the new Intercontinental Hotel in Mumbai, which was part of the Taj Group of more than sixty luxury hotels. Mr Haroun, who was Vice President of Intercontinental Hotels, introduced me to Ajit Kerkar, the managing director of Taj. Some years later Mr Kerkar contacted me and came to visit my own more modest operation of Royal Sweets in the UK, but he was impressed enough by my track record to put a proposal to me.

"Why don't we do the same thing but also with frozen Indian food in America?" he asked. It was an idea I had been mulling over for some time although I had in mind opening a business in Canada. But Mr Kerkar already had a successful restaurant called RAGA in New York and he persuaded me that America was the right place to start. The idea was to prepare frozen Indian meals and supply direct to restaurants and supermarkets as well as selling the sweets. At the time there were more than 800,000 Indian immigrants in the USA.

It was a bold idea to try to sell large quantities of Indian food to the Americans. The opportunity of working closely with the Taj Group of hotels enchanted me; the mere fact that a man like Mr Kerkar should even consider working with me boosted my ego as high as it could possibly go. So I jumped at the chance, and the following year, leaving a trusted team in charge in the UK, I moved to New York to establish the operation, commuting back to England to keep an eye on the UK business.

We formed a company that bought Lufthansa's flight kitchen in Queens opposite La Guardia airport. It was virtually purpose-built for our needs, with appropriate infrastructure apart from the technical side, and in just a few short months we started manufacturing Indian sweets and frozen meals. The idea was that we would manufacture, and not dabble in selling but find a retailer. But we tried to do both. The food was excellent, the technology was first class, but we allowed our attention to be diverted. We tried to get the food into supermarkets in the predominantly Indian-populated areas – or indeed into any takers – as well as distributing to the seven restaurants that we opened in quick succession: first in Manhattan, then in Queens, Connecticut and Long Island, all within a year.

I remember the opening night of our first restaurant in midtown Manhattan. It was very exciting; I had come from a shop in Mumbai, then to shops in London, and now here I was opening my own restaurant in New York. I was a young man and my confidence was running high. Who wouldn't be excited? We organised parties for the elite members of the local Asian community. We were targeting the Asians but we also hoped to expand the clientele to include the Americans, introducing them to the delights of Indian cuisine. I believe I did everything humanly possible to make a success of the enterprise.

It seemed to be a success. The restaurant was packed for the opening night and business was sufficiently brisk over the following days for us to think that we were onto a winner. It was certainly only a matter of weeks before we began planning our second opening, and then our third and fourth, until we had nine in all. The reality was that the first restaurant was not a huge triumph, but we convinced ourselves that it was just a question of exposure: if we had more restaurants out there they would be able to promote one another.

I used to visit two or three of the restaurants every day, checking on the service and of course – remembering my training back in the Crawford Market sweet shop – keeping an eye on the books. At first things all appeared to be on track. Business was fair without being outstanding, which we put down to people just getting used to new tastes. The food looked good and we met the stringent US food regulations. The factory was operating well and we were employing about fifty people. We even started exporting some of our frozen products back to England!

I should have picked up the message sooner. Here was I, thousands of miles away, making food to send back home. It is easy to be wise after the event, and the only advice I can pass on is to keep alert to all the signals you are receiving: do not have such tunnel vision that you cannot see what is going on around you. But I was on a mission to crack America, the land of opportunity. Many of my own friends from India had gone straight there and been successful, and I was convinced that I would do the same. Young people sometimes have to go through the pain of experience before the penny finally drops. The premises were all rented so there was no chance of my benefiting from any rise in the freehold value. All the time expenses were mounting, and much of the business was funded by Taj.

Perhaps I was trying to spread myself too thinly, but the reality was that our concept for the frozen Indian meals did not work. We were twenty-five years too early – America is still not really ready for it even today in 2008. In those days there were only a few Indian restaurants in the States. We had used the Taj infrastructure to put the word out but it was not what I would call proper, thorough marketing. We had not given enough thought to the way Americans buy their food, or indeed where they buy their food. They have large supermarkets, of course, but they can also buy from local stores, which seem to provide everything from pharmaceuticals to foodstuffs. It was not good enough just to sell to the local Asian population: we had to reach the indigenous American consumer, and that was a hurdle too far. We were trying to emulate what the Japanese were doing with their noodle chains, but New York in 1980 was not the place for chicken curries.

It only took two more years for all the restaurants to close and for us to wind up the business. It was an expensive disaster. My message to all young entrepreneurs is do your research properly; make sure you have a market. It does not matter how good your product is, how authentic the ingredients or even how slick your production: if no one wants to buy what you are selling, you are finished before you have begun. Even if you sell gold for the price of silver, if no one wants gold it is worthless. Hindsight is a wonderful thing, but what we should have done was start with one restaurant and see how it did before racing ahead. In London when we opened our first shop at 92 Broadway, which is still there, I tested the pulse of the market and only then expanded. My expansion in the UK was achieved on the basis of ready buyers. Marketing is vital. America was not ready. No matter how good our food was, no matter how efficient our production and service was, we simply had no market.

Interestingly, we had one franchised sweet shop, which was doing very well, but America is a huge country and the Asian population was widely scattered, making it a difficult market to corner. Americans did not want to eat Indian food. We suffered heavy losses and this was without doubt the biggest mistake of my career. Whatever I had earned in the UK I lost in America – all my savings. The only silver lining was the relationship I established with one new client that we picked up: Waitrose in England, who were taking our frozen meals from America. We had to lose them at the time, but they remembered me and later they would become one of the major customers of Noon Products.

Mr Kerkar, who is a powerful man, did not want to admit defeat at first and continued with the business for a little longer after I left but he only lost more money before finally abandoning the idea himself. When the writing is on the wall it is best to accept it and move on. I learned in American the expression that there is no point in flogging a dead horse!

In the meantime Taj had invited me to get involved in their hotel business. When they wanted to buy some more hotels both in America and in England I was able to help by introducing them to some wealthy Indians who put the equity into the scheme. In London they bought St James Court in Buckingham Gate and I was made a director. In America they bought the Lexington Hotel and five other hotels in Washington; again I was made a director and also Vice President.

But my heart was in the food business, which was not doing well. I was a little uncomfortable despite the fact that Taj treated me very well, particularly Ajit Kerkar himself. I was given a very nice office in the Lexington Hotel, I was able to stay in his daughter's vacant apartment as she had completed her studies and was returning to India, and I was given a car. However, one day when we were on a visit to India I told him that I would like to go back to England where my Bombay Halwa operation needed my input even though I was already travelling back to the UK every month or so. Ajit Kerkar was very upset and tried to persuade me not to take such a hasty step. He said I was mad to walk away from a huge conglomerate like Taj Hotels, and all for a tiny business in London. I remember the day – it was 28 September 1982, my daughter Zeenat's birthday. I told my friend Kerkar that he had taught me too well. I reminded him that he was an entrepreneur and when he was running just one hotel and the Tata empire who owned it suggested to him that it should be turned into an office block, he had stubbornly refused. How right he had been. He eventually grew that single hotel into a chain of seventy. I too was stubborn and wanted to build my own small empire.

I had made up my mind and, in reality, I was not cut out to be a corporate animal. Taj was a large company, and it was a bit like working in the civil service. You either thrive in that sort of environment – climbing the ladder, fighting for promotion, actually enjoying the committees and round table discussions, sending memos back and forth – or you don't. If I am given a pile of papers to read I will glance at them but always in the end I rely on my instinct. Both paths are perfectly legitimate, but you must recognise quickly where you fit and where you are comfortable. You only have one life and you have got to be true to yourself. The question every young person must ask themselves is: "Do I have the confidence to go it alone and take charge or am I more comfortable in the corporate world of democratic votes and collective board decisions?" Of course, even if you are the former type, like me, you may still find yourself with a board of directors, and it would be foolish not to listen to their advice, but if you have the majority vote at least you can steer your committee towards your goals.

So with my tail somewhat between my legs and surrendering part of my equity in the Taj Group, I returned to England in 1984. At the back of my mind I thought that maybe England was the right place to launch the Indian meals concept to a wider public, and so it would prove to be. I believe there are geographical and historical reasons why Indian food works in the UK.

It is successful because the British Crown ruled India for many decades, and before that it was administered by the East India Company. This could not have happened without the culture and influences of the land being to some extent absorbed. The English language itself is full of words derived from India. The British Isles are also physically closer to India than is America, which is eighteen hours' flying time away as opposed to the eight hours it takes to get to the UK. And lastly, whatever views one might hold about the British Raj, when the English left India they left as friends.

My American odyssey had not been entirely wasted. Before going to America I had been preparing specialised sweets in relatively small quantities. What I had learned in New York was all about the preparation of bulk meals using the very latest technology without losing the traditional value or quality of the food.

I could have been disheartened by the failure in America and stuck with Royal Sweets, focusing my efforts on building that business, but I knew the UK was where frozen and chilled Indian meals, straight from the factory to the supermarket, could work. At the time there were about 7500 Indian restaurants in the UK; now there are 10,000 or more. I said to myself that one day this Indian food would land on the supermarket shelves with a vengeance – and it did.

Do I have any regrets about America? Of course I regret the loss of money, but regrets are non-productive, and if I look at the "balance sheet" of my American venture, and include all the knowledge I gained about technology and bulk production, I would say the books at least balance. I also made many friends and what would turn out to be a major client for the future. America was all part of my continuing learning experience – it is just that sometimes we have to learn painful lessons! There is no question, however, that America is indeed a land of opportunity, and I love their "can do" philosophy. They have a tremendous energy and enthusiasm for their work and also their play. Playtime is important, and if you want twenty-four-hour entertainment New York is the place to be. Like the rest of America I put in long hours at work, but because the business was not going well I was worried and did not find it easy to relax. Failure was staring me in the face and Bombay Halwa in the UK was not progressing as well as it might have been. So there was tremendous tension – at least for me. And there was work for me at home in England. The UK is the best country in the world in which to do business – it is a pluralistic society of essentially gentle people. I will remain alert, however, to what America or indeed any other land might still have to offer me in the future.

Personally, I also loved and lost again as a result of my trip to America. I met a charming lady in New York called Ruxana Kardar, who came from a very eminent family. Her father was a well-known film producer and director in Mumbai. We were both divorcees and both with two daughters. We soon married and had a very happy life in America before returning together to England. But – and here is a note of caution to others like me who marry for a second time – when you and your spouse have children from previous marriages you are not entitled to assume that just because you get along as a couple your children will necessarily like one another. They have their own personalities too. Ruxana's daughters were delightful; my daughters were just from a different background. From time to time conflicts would arise and inevitably I would take the side of my daughters and Ruxana would side with her girls. That is normal, and no blame whatsoever could be placed on the children. In fact Ruxana's daughters were living with their father in Hyderabad and I was instrumental in getting them to come to live with us and to complete their education in the West. Later I helped Ruxana's eldest girl, Farneck, get a job with Taj – I was delighted to help. On paper everything was perfect, but you cannot just put two families together in one house and say: "Right, from now on everyone will get along." It does not work.

In the end we decided to part, although Ruxana continues to live in the UK. So my message to people considering marrying again is simply to be careful when there are children involved. You cannot dictate a relationship to children. Do not be so selfish as to say: "Well, we two love each other – you children just sort it out." It does not work, particularly in the Asian culture.

Chapter Seven

My 'Eureka' Moment

It would be wrong to give the impression that Royal Sweets UK was in any way an old, forgotten project. Far from it: it continues to be a thriving business for me today, but not one that hits the headlines.

Since it started in the early 1970s as the original UK producer of Indian sweets and savoury mixes under the Royal and Bombay Food brands, Bombay Halwa Limited, the parent company, has diversified in several ways. While I was still in the States we opened a dedicated flight kitchen to serve the aviation catering industry in 1982 and by the end of 2004 we would have a brand new purpose-built 20,000 square foot flight kitchen, which was commissioned and approved by the UK Halal Food Authority. We have been supplying Asian vegetarian meals to leading airlines for more than twenty-five years.

The wide range of authentic snacks, savoury mixes, chutneys, desserts, kulfi and ice creams is continuously evolving. One of my proudest and best-known inventions is Bombay Mix, which is available in bars everywhere. A dark moment was when I heard that the European Commission wanted to change the name to Mumbai Mix. They will have to fight me in the courts over that one!

Although I was focused on developing the Bombay Halwa business, opening more franchise shops between 1984 and 1989, I knew fairly soon after my return to England that I would have to find a new project. After all the family was growing. My older daughter, Zeenat, was married to Arun Harnal. In 1986 her daughter, Natania, was born in London, so far my only grandchild and the apple of my eye.

I did my own personal stock-take to decide what that should be. I knew about food, I knew about the packaging required for bulk supplies and I knew about the technology of mass production of high-quality food. The breakthrough came when I went shopping.

One weekend I went down to my local supermarket and noticed the packets of ready-to-eat curries. Needless to say, in the past I had not even given such products a second glance as every self-respecting Indian family always prepares their own meals at home. But I decided to buy all the different so-called Indian meals on offer. They were the boil-in-the-bag variety, and as far removed from what I considered to be real Indian food as it was possible to get. They were insipid, badly packaged and poorly presented. No one, not even the poorest person in India, would consider anything on offer as an authentic Indian meal. They ended up in the bin. This was my own "Eureka!" moment, when I realised what could be done and had the courage to back my own instincts. I was sure people would buy my meals if they were at least as good as the food they could buy in a restaurant.

I am a food man. I like cooking for friends when they come round and I will cook a couple of dishes every weekend. So fired up once again I took out a large loan on a second mortgage on my house. I incorporated Noon Products Limited and bought a 5500 square foot site also in Southall, and I took on eleven employees. What we needed was the latest technology, but that simply didn't exist for bulk processing of Indian food. So we had to make our own prototype and experiment with the design. Naturally we made a few mistakes along the way, which cost money, but eventually we got it right.

I didn't realise it at the time but I was about to turn a nation of fish and chips and roast beef eaters into curry fanatics. As for competition, there wasn't any: boil-in-the-bag was not even the same dish, and it certainly had nothing to do with India as far as I was concerned. I deliberately set my sights high. Quality and absolute authenticity would be my watchwords, just as they had been in Royal Sweets, and there could be no compromise:

either the English palate would adapt to genuine Indian flavours or the business would sink without trace.

I hired a brilliant chef – Ashok Kaul – who was responsible for Air India meals and we started experimenting: buying food from all the supermarkets, tasting, and asking ourselves whether we would ever eat what was on offer. The answer was an emphatic no. So I began to believe that I might have found a genuine niche market in the food industry.

My friends all agreed, and they advised me to produce packed meals, hire two or three vans and start selling to all the Indian corner shops in London. But I said to myself that was exactly what I was not going to do. My first contract was with one of the major airlines to provide in-flight meals, but I was after a bigger target. I wanted to produce in bulk, so I decided that I would approach the largest frozen food distributor in this country at the time, Birds Eye, which was owned by the mighty Unilever. I didn't stand a chance. There I was, a tiny start-up operation called Noon Products, approaching Birds Eye, who were themselves manufacturing boil-in-the-bag Indian food that could best be described as a messy affair. The idea was summarily dismissed. You could almost hear my friends saying: "We told you so – you should have taken our advice and approached the multitude of little Indian corner shops."

Eventually, after a few months of constant nagging, Birds Eye agreed that perhaps I had something they didn't: namely, real Indian food, well packaged and well cooked. Instead of food that slopped about in a bag and invariably spilled off the plate when you tried to cut the bag open after it was plucked from a boiling saucepan, I had developed attractive packaging with trays of food that could be cooked in a microwave or a conventional oven. Birds Eye could not argue. At last, we were about to receive our first order, which we knew would be a modest request as we were entirely untested. We thought we would be lucky if it was worth £100,000. So we were stunned when eventually the call came through: they wanted to place an order for three meal varieties worth £2.7 million. I nearly fell off my chair. This was in February 1989.

The truth of the matter was that we were novices in the businesses, and although Birds Eye had helped us develop the micro-biological controls, we messed up. The first batch of 38,000 meals we rejected ourselves on what you might call the "bug count". This measures the micro-organisms in the food. But we could not just throw out the food because it was in Birds Eye packaging, so the batch actually received a burial certificate because it was incinerated by the public health office. It was a setback to say the least, and poor Ashok, the head chef, was very upset. I tried to cheer him up and told him not to worry – we would write it off as a start-up cost of our operation. It was not just Ashok who was upset: all the workforce plus my entire family had been drafted in to help meet the order We started all over again. That quantity takes about fifteen days to produce, and the days and weeks just blurred into one.

The next batch was perfect and soon our Birds Eye products were really taking off. This was the first time in Britain that the public had seen authentic Indian food in supermarkets. There were three dishes: beef rogan josh, chicken korma and chicken makhanwala – I thought this last name was a little too complicated so I changed the name to chicken tikka masala, which I am proud to say is practically the UK's new national dish. We could not produce enough even though we were now operating out of a 5500 square foot factory built to Birds Eye's specification.

Birds Eye called me and said we were not fulfilling our contract. Apparently their customers could not get enough of our meals – it was a good problem to have. We had just eighty employees to begin with so I offered to start working on Sundays as well and Birds Eye agreed to pay extra to cover the overtime. Quite simply, that was how Noon Products took off. The workforce rapidly expanded and we launched some new menus. The great British public – at least those who shopped at supermarkets for Birds Eye products – had readily adopted the new exotic meals. We were working flat out.

I have to say I felt vindicated for my stubborn insistence on quality and authenticity, and also for aiming for the top of the market. At the very least I could say I was on the right track. The easy, safe option would have been to fill up my own vans and hawk the products round the Indian outlets, but that would have been thinking small and I was certain curry could be sold to all Britons and not just Indians. It also pays not to give up. Birds

Eye's senior brand manager probably thought the only way that he could stop this pest calling his office for an appointment was to see him once and send him on his way, but full credit to him for accepting that there was a better way to serve Indian food. The foray into America had also paid dividends. By investing in the latest technology, we were not only able to maintain the highest possible standards of food quality and hygiene but were also able to meet demand – even if it meant that the whole family had to turn up at the factory every day of the week to deliver on our commitment.

Word travels fast, and in the world of supermarkets faster than in most, so it was not long before Sainsbury's scouts had noticed what was happening to Birds Eye Indian meals. Within a matter of months I had a phone call inviting me to meet David Sainsbury (now Lord Sainsbury) and his team.

I learned in the food business, which I have been in since I was a boy, always to ask for an appointment between 12 noon and 1 p.m., when the people you have come to see have not yet had lunch and therefore are hungry. So I asked for a 12 noon appointment. I took Ashok Kaul, my head chef and production manager, with me and a selection of foods. Not only was David Sainsbury there but so too were many board members. I was quite surprised. There was Tom Vyner, Bob Cooper and the head of the prepared chill food department.

David Sainsbury got straight to the point. He said: "We are also selling Indian food and we are selling about £750,000 a year, which is a lot. What do you think about our food?"

In my reckless way, which I strongly urge other young entrepreneurs not to emulate because while I got away with it they might not, I said: "Mr Sainsbury, I don't think you should be selling this food because I think it is rubbish." It was all or nothing tactics. They were taken aback by this upstart and said: "All right, let's have a look at your food."

I asked for a microwave and Ashok prepared probably the most important meal of his and my life. We watched in silence as they tasted. I think it is safe to say that they were impressed, and I am not surprised, for three reasons: it was different, it was authentic and, crucially, they were hungry. They said they would give us a try, but I was producing frozen food for Birds Eye and they asked me to develop chilled food. Their technical department visited my factory and they were aghast to see that my factory was too small for them. I could see the order slipping through my fingers.

They said: "You don't have dedicated high- and low-risk areas." What they meant was that when you cook the food you are dealing with the raw materials and that is low risk. Then it is transferred to packaging and that is high risk. The two groups of people must not come into contact with each other. So they rejected my plant. It was a disaster. The factory was too small and the stringent hygiene requirements demanded by Sainsbury were not met.

Bob Cooper, one of the board members at the meeting and like me a great risk taker, called me. Deeply apologetic and crestfallen, I said: "I am sorry I can't help it that my plant is too small, but give me a chance and we will take maximum care and in less than a year's time we will buy a new place with dedicated high- and low-risk areas."

He called the technical department and uttered the key words. He said: "The commercial consideration will prevail." Those five simple words saved us. He told his technical people that he wanted them to work with us and get Noon Products off the ground. He said we should be allowed to use the same factory and the same production methods in order to start the process; other technical changes could follow later but nothing should get in the way of that first order. "Commercial consideration will prevail" should be every company's motto: not only does it make complete business sense, but it is also common sense and very much the American can-do approach that I had experienced previously.

I went home happy and then had to set up a meeting with the buyers. They had no idea of authentic Indian food and they tried to influence us by saying we should have sultanas and apple pieces in our curries. I know this is how a lot of English people enjoyed their curry, but it is not the real thing. I said that was exactly what I was not going to do, because sultanas and apples are incongruous in curries and the concept I was married to was authenticity. I said I would sell by authenticity or I would sink by it. So the buyers left disappointed. Once again this awkward chap was not following orders, and they reported to the board.

This time an exasperated Bob Cooper came to see me and said: "What are you doing? We solve one problem and you create another." I said: "Bob, my problem is that my product is authentic and I am not going to use anything that is not authentic. My product will be exactly as the Indian housewife makes it and follow the housewife's recipe." Perhaps he was impressed by my reluctance to waver from my convictions, or perhaps he was giving me just enough rope to hang myself – after all, he had agreed to all my demands, and if the project failed there was no one to blame but myself. He told his buying team: "Relax, let him do what he wants." We were on our way now, supplying to Sainsbury's 500 outlets, and today Noon Products is the only brand that is allowed to carry its own name on the back of Sainsbury's packaging. I have been fortunate to work with all the heads at Sainsbury's over the years, the two Lords John and David Sainsbury, then Dino Adriano, Sir Peter Davis and latterly Justin King, a young, dynamic force who has maintained the stature of the company.

The third major customer to come our way was Waitrose. In fact they were old friends from my days in New York, when I used to send them container-loads of frozen food from America to the UK. Unfortunately the exchange rate worked against us, and when the pound and dollar reached parity it no longer made commercial sense to continue. But I kept in touch with them and that same year, 1989, they too began stocking our product.

Before long we had about 35,000 square feet producing millions of pre-prepared curries every year. Crucially, I also bought another 30,000 square feet for warehousing and storage. This would prove to have been a critical decision about six years later when disaster struck.

We had gone from zero to a turnover of £16 million in five years. I soon earned the dubious title of "Curry King" in the press – a phrase coined by the *Daily Telegraph* journalist, Amit Roy, who has been following the ups and downs of my career in the UK almost from the day I arrived in the country. I have the honour of being one of the first people to inspire the English people to acquire a love of curry through the supermarket shelves – the late Robin Cook, former Labour Foreign Secretary, said chicken tikka masala had indeed become the new national dish. One TV cook and food critic,

Roopa Gulati, paid me the nicest compliment: "Noon has brought dignity to formula curries."

Should there have been any doubt, some years later the Lord Mayor of London had a benevolent lunch for the army in Guildhall on 24 April 2008 that was attended by the Prince of Wales. I supplied the lunch for 1000 people and of course it was a curry lunch. We prepared and chilled the meals, and took them to Guildhall where my team of chefs cooked and prepared everything. Army mess people served it. Curry in Guildhall! Britain's eating habits have come a long way.

I would like to pay tribute, though, to the Bangladeshi community who were the real pioneers of bringing Indian food to the UK. I always say that in those days Indian restaurants were synonymous with garish decor, flock wallpaper and powerful aroma. You invariably had to take your clothes to the dry cleaners after every meal. But times have changed. The British public has become more discerning and understands the difference between different regional Indian cuisines – they know their tikka masala from their chicken korma. Two and a half million people are said to eat curry in Britain every year, generating sales of over £3 billion, and there is even a glitzy British Curry Awards.

Strictly speaking, of course, curry only means "gravy", but that is nitpicking and everyone knows what "going out for a curry" means. I once said that the British conquered India with gunpowder in the nineteenth century and Indians returned the compliment 100 years later conquering Britain with curry powder. Also, if we are being strictly accurate, we should not just refer to "Indian restaurants" because curry comes from the whole of the Asian region. And that brings me to my chefs – perhaps my prize investment. I have a number of chefs, each of them from a different part of India and every one top of their field; they can not only produce a dish from any region in India but can also prepare an authentic recipe from many other parts of the world. The point is that our customers might want a Thai, Moroccan, Chinese or European meal and we can produce it. The backbone of Noon Products, I must stress, is my team of chefs: Ashok Kaul, Rameshbabu Chonath, B. Sainath Rao and about twenty other talented individuals.

The irony of it all is that I do not think India herself is ready for my products. While in the UK we produce between 300,000 and 350,000 meals, six days a week, to keep up with demand that produced a turnover in excess of £150 million in 2006/7, the same market does not exist in India. The other problem is the lack of a "cold chain" in India, which would be essential if we were to introduce our ready meals there. The food has to be stored at a specific temperature that must be maintained by the trucks that take the meals to the retail outlets – that network of trucks does not exist, and nor probably do the supermarkets with the correct chill cabinets. In fact even in the relatively sophisticated western world, the importance of maintaining the "cold chain" cannot be overemphasised. There is no point buying chilled food then putting it in the boot of your car while you go shopping for an hour and still expecting the ideal temperature of the food to be maintained – all of which emphasises the difficulty of reaching a predominantly rural market like India. But who knows? One day I might even be able to sell curries to Indians in India.

Since we are talking about food, it only seems right to mention two stories about individuals who in their own way have helped my business to succeed. One of the most amazing stories is about a man called Intisar Husain who in 1990 was doing odd jobs including some work for Bombay Halwa Limited. One day he came to my office and said he didn't want to be doing odd jobs all his life. He's a very nice man, and an honourable man of impeccable character and integrity. He was from Pakistan and had lived in Germany for some years before moving to England. He asked if there was something he could do for me. At that stage we were building a new unit and so he became a builder – he had building experience. He got his relations and friends to work on the factory and when it was complete he asked what else I needed him to do. I told him I bought almost 2 tonnes of chicken a day. If I gave him a place, would he start dicing the chicken for me? He said he had never done that sort of work and I replied that – well – I had never sold ready meals before.

But he was an adventurous man so he started hand-cutting and dicing, and as Noon Products grew, he grew. I was also buying prepared vegetables from another supplier at the time. One day, unannounced, I went to see the operation and wasn't impressed. They were buying low-quality vegetables at a cheap price, cutting off the rotten part and using the rest, but charging the same price as for good-quality vegetables. So I asked Intisar if he would take on the preparation of vegetables as well, and I gave him some more space. By then we were using 30 tonnes of chicken a day or more. You can't ask people to cut that quantity by hand, so we encouraged him to buy an American cutting machine that used water jets. He bought two, each one worth £1 million. Eventually he was able to buy the plant he was using from me. Today he is a millionaire, drives an expensive car and has about 200 people working for him, supplying exclusively to us. Our families are extremely close. He took advantage of our friendship and delivered, and I am so proud of him.

The second remarkable story inevitably has a cricketing angle! There were three brothers, Ilias, Ejaz and Afzal Husain. We used to play cricket together most Sundays in the summer. Their business, Spurways, based in Wembley, was selling samosas. One Sunday the eldest brother came to me and asked for help in introducing their product to Sainsbury's. So we went to see their plant. It was not very well organised and they only had a turnover of £4000 a week. But I agreed to give them a plan and got my technical people involved. The brothers implemented the plan and then I agreed to bring the Sainsbury's people to have a look and try to persuade them to give the company some business. To cut a long story short, the first order Sainsbury's placed was for £25,000 a week. That business grew so fast that they also ran out of space, so I helped them buy another plot of land in Greenford, West London, and again I got our technical people to help them. In 2005 we bought them out and integrated their plant into our business. All they were doing was finger food, but all credit to them. They had worked hard and built the company up from nothing. This is what makes working worthwhile.

Chapter Eight

'You Get Out What You Put In'

Today we have over 1400 employees in Noon Products, preparing millions of meals every month for leading outlets including Sainsbury's, Waitrose, Marks & Spencer, Budgens, Lidl, Morrisons and Somerfield, and we also export to Europe, Hong Kong and the Middle East. The heart of the business is the ingredients we use in the meals we produce, and although I don't do so much of it today, one of my most self-indulgent pleasures – I could hardly call it work – is the research. Most of our spices come from India. It makes a big difference in the quality, which is vital to help us maintain our 40 per cent market share in the ready-made Indian food sector. What is particularly satisfying is that so much of this market share is at the top end, which is testimony to the nature of our customer base.

I hope you will forgive me if I indulge myself a little here to explain how and where we source our ingredients and how we prepare our meals. I am passionate, of course, about food and love to cook for family and friends when I can. I remember meals being prepared as far back as when I was a boy watching my mother peeling fresh prawns. If nothing else I hope this chapter will whet your a appetite, not only to have a good meal (Indian of course) but maybe even to start cooking yourself.

We have to thank the Great Moghul emperors who ruled India for 300 years for many of the culinary delights that have emerged. They supported cooks, lavished their patronage on them and allowed them to explore and be creative. And as I have said many times before – without a trace of embarrassment – they raised Indian cuisine to the level of an art form. In a land of a billion people you would expect some variety, but broadly you could say that the food ranges from the so-called Moghlai cuisine of the North, named after the Grand Moghuls and famed for its richness and grandeur, to the vegetarian recipes of Chennai (formerly Madras), in which rice and lentils (dal) are central to the diet, to the fish dishes of the South West along the Malabar coastline. For thousands of years merchants and invaders, carried on the monsoon winds, sailed these coastal waters in search of prizes. The Portuguese explorer Vasco da Gama, in the fifteenth century, followed the voyages of the Egyptians and Romans before him. Today cooking in the state of Kerala on India's south-western coastline reflects the influence of all these visitors – Christians, Jews and Muslims. Chief among the prizes were the spices used in medicine and perfumery as well as in cooking. If you ever doubted that there was art in cooking, just visit a spice market where the colours if not the aroma will stun you.

Travelling in search of new spices and new recipes with my chefs is one of the ultimate perks of the job and is always a journey of thrilling discovery. Over the years we have visited every corner of India and have never failed to find yet another jewel, often being prepared in the simplest of kitchens over a basic stove. When I started in this business my guide was to ask what housewives use in their cooking. Do they use artificial flavouring or additives? No, they use natural products. Fortunately I already had a great enthusiasm for and enjoyment of cooking and I modelled everything I did, both at home and in my factories, on my enthusiasms. In a word, I cherished authenticity, and I believe that is what appealed to my first crucial customers.

There are many stories of how we came across some of these culinary gems but I will recall just a couple. Whenever I go somewhere to eat, with friends or when I am travelling through India, I always pay close attention to what I am eating. If I like a particular meal, even today, I ask my hostess or her chef how the food was prepared – What did you use? At what stage in the preparation did you put in the spices? – and I make a mental note and later write it in my diary. But I am fortunate because I have this passion for food. It is not just a business, and when my chefs see this passion they also rise to the occasion. I do not just tell them to make this meal or that meal. I like to tell them about any new discoveries I have made and I am genuinely interested in their creations. It is a bit like being an antiques collector who cannot keep out of the shops he discovers.

I remember on one occasion when I was on my own at home I made what I thought was a brilliant chicken curry, but I made it very thick and I said to myself that I would convert it into biriani. So I prepared some rice, added the chicken and started steaming it. It turned out to be divine! I always tell my chefs about what I have been cooking and they are extremely patient with me! To me chefs are artists, and I was fortunate in finding Ashok Kaul, a brilliantly quick learner able to combine his vast knowledge of food with the latest technology that I introduced to him. He is always ready to explore new techniques even if it means using apparently harsh-looking modern equipment that he fears might ruin his delicate vegetables.

I am extremely partial to turmeric. When I cook at home I use a lot – not because of its medicinal qualities (it is particularly helpful with Alzheimer's, I believe) but because of its unique flavour. I use it more than housewives do. I went to a town called Kohlapur, which is not far from Mumbai, where they produce the best turmeric in the whole of India. I started a company in Mumbai called Noon Consultancy Limited just to ship this spice. Now anything we want from the whole of India they supply. My brother in law, Moiz Challawalla, was retiring as CEO of New Standard Engineering, a large company. He was sixty-five years old, and a brilliant man, and I persuaded him that this was a perfect opportunity for us both. So I bought an office in Central Mumbai and I said: "Let's start." Neither of us really knew what we would be doing or where this little office was going apart from ordering the turmeric. But expand it did.

We began our search for suppliers of all the other spices we use, and Moiz and I, sometimes with our head chef, would travel all over the country applying a combination of business acumen and quality control. I used my nose, and I have a clean, clear palate. Then I would ask myself if our head of quality control back in England would accept it. We would send samples back to London, where the chefs would taste them and our laboratories would test and analyse them from a micro-biological point of view and only then, once a sample had been accepted, did we place an order. Turmeric is not just turmeric: it varies enormously from place to place – what you buy in the shops is quite different from the raw ingredient we use. It is this attention to detail and quality that I believe sets us apart. In whatever dish you make, whether it is Indian, Chinese or whatever, it is the quality of the ingredients that makes the dish.

Following on from the spices, our little Noon Consultancy was soon handling all sorts of other supplies, including stainless steel trays, which were both good quality and cheap, and all the granite we used in one of our new factories.

Having made the initial discovery, the skill of my chefs is to translate the housewife's recipe into a meal that can be reproduced in its thousands without losing any of its authenticity. But preparing an authentic Indian meal is a cumbersome and detailed process and somehow we have to automate the system. We do that by replicating the best Indian cooking practices in a process we designed ourselves after much trial and error. It is all "high-tech" but it was only approved because it preserved the authenticity of the meal. Some chefs have an aversion to science. In place of the traditional cylindrical clay tandoor oven we have a 30-metre-long conveyor belt that carries the food into turbo-ovens we designed ourselves, preparing the chicken in precisely nine minutes. We cook rice in 500-tonne batches and use about 30 tonnes of onions every day, and our sauces are prepared in giant kettles using stirrers driven by computers. But – and it is a big but – the flavours and the spices and the final taste are controlled by my chefs, who undergo two years' training with us. We have designed, for example, special ovens and, yes, much of the production is computer-controlled – to deliver consistency on such a scale, as well as authenticity, it has to be – but the secret of getting the meals just right, according to our chefs, is the sequence in which you add the spices. The flavours come out at different times in the preparation of the dish.

Another vital stage in the preparation of many dishes is marinating, but of course we cannot afford the luxury of leaving meat to gently soak up all the succulent juices for hours on end, particularly as we also use some eighty different marinades – quite apart from hygiene considerations. Here again science comes to our aid. On a visit to a German food factory I noticed what they called a "meat massager". It sounds a bit grim, but what it was doing was tenderising the meat by spinning it at high speed – 500 pounds at a time – until all the pores were effectively loosened. When I got home I experimented with the idea, pouring the marinade into the machine. The experiment was a success, allowing me to marinate the food perfectly and giving in 30 minutes an effect that would have taken twenty-four hours using conventional methods. I know it might strike people as being a bit mechanical but I defy anyone to tell the difference in the result.

I like to think that if I could arrange a blind tasting of one of our products with the originator of the recipe, perhaps still today bent over her oven in a remote village of India, she would not be able to taste the difference. My friend Delia Smith, the famous TV chef and also a fellow trustee on the British Food Trust, once invited some friends round to her house for supper and served them various Noon products without saying a word. Happily they were all very complimentary and assumed Delia had cooked the meal herself. Only at the end of the meal did she reveal its origin, explaining that the meal was part of some research she was doing for an article. At least we did not let her down.

Once our recipes have been minutely researched, every single meal with all the ingredients is listed in our handbooks with the exact portions for each one. I would not even think about changing the levels by 0.01 per cent. Precision is everything. We check every batch on a regular basis: it only takes one mistake to ruin a reputation. I think we have some of the most stringent hygiene regimes in the business. Today we have our own microbiological laboratory where qualified staff test raw materials and products. We also have spot checks on the hygiene of all parts of the factory as well as the staff. We even have metal detectors checking the raw materials on the way into the factory and more metal detectors checking the finished products on the way out.

Some things you cannot replicate, no matter how sophisticated the technology. We imported a traditional stone spice grinder from India, just for some of our Goan recipes. This is not a gimmick – it is the only way we can ensure that the spices are at their freshest when they go into the food.

Our recipes may contain between thirty and forty different ingredients and our workers have to have three or four years' experience before they are allowed to make the sauces.

Not surprisingly, we are the largest users of fresh garlic, coriander and ginger in the country. We also get through many tonnes of onions, rice, lamb, prawns and chicken every day. You cannot be authentic without authentic ingredients. We have a high consumption of rice, cereal and cashew nuts as well as of spices. We rely on the services of suppliers such as Tilda Rice and Moni Verma's Veetee Rice who use only the finest products, such as basmati rice from the foothills of the Himalayas. Moni became a close fiend of mine, we supported each other in our businesses and he was particularly vocal in a positive manner when I later had some political difficulties, giving press interviews while a few of my friends who had known me for a long time managed to dodge the journalists' calls.

Quality of products is not just a marketing tool but the pursuit of excellence and quality that I have applied since my youth when I worked in the family sweetshops and that continues to this day in everything I do. The expression "you get out what you put in" applies to everything in life.

But before we take ourselves too seriously, it is worth remembering when debating authenticity that the great chicken tikka masala was probably invented in the English Midlands, albeit in an Indian restaurant. I always say that is irrelevant – the dish still contains Indian spices. And I did not know what a balti was before I went to Birmingham! But there is no law that says you should only eat an Indian meal if it was invented in India. I once said that food has no religion or no nationality. Wherever you go in the world you see the French eating Italian food, the Japanese eating Indian food: it is all food, and if you like it, eat it.

By the end of each working day we have produced more than 300,000 meals drawn from approximately 300 different recipes. Most are Indian, of course, but we also have Mexican, Thai, Chinese, Malaysian, Italian and traditional British and also low-fat dishes.

Of course quantity is not the key parameter, quality is everything. Dame Deidre Hutton, chairman of the Food Standards Agency, visited our factory and was so impressed that she invited me to give a talk to her own staff. I told them that one can pass all the legislation one likes but you have to understand the practicalities of implementing the rules at factory floor level. That message was received so well that the FSA sent someone on secondment to Noon Products to see the difficulties faced on a daily basis. If Noon Products is the crowning glory of my business life, this 'accolade' from the FSA of making us a benchmark for the preparation of food, was incredible. For nearly 20 years we have strived to maintain those standards.

On the subject of eating curry, do I practise what I preach? I would say I eat curry at least every other day, and my favourites are lamb and chicken curries. They say that the average English family eats a curry once every ten days, which is good news! If I were asked where you could find the best curry in the world I would say, perhaps not surprisingly, in North India. Actually, most of the meals people eat in the UK are based on North Indian recipes, although we search the length and breadth of the country for new dishes. Each region has its own speciality and favourite ingredients – for example, cream and yoghurt in Delhi, and coconut in the coastal areas. The mistake many people who are frightened of trying a curry make is thinking that because it is spicy it has to be hot. That is a fallacy, although it did become something of a badge of honour among young men in Britain to see how strong a curry they could eat. Personally I prefer mild curries because I feel I can enjoy the flavours more, but it is a matter of choice.

Chapter Nine

The Tiger Roars

By the mid 1990s I was beginning to enjoy the good things in life. My other company, Bombay Halwa, was doing reasonably well and Noon Products was doing exceedingly well. I had been honoured by my fellow Asians by being named Asian of the Year in 1994. The award was presented by the Rt Hon. Michael Heseltine, then President of the Board of Trade, and I received kind messages of congratulations from the Prime Minister, John Major, and Paddy Ashdown, leader of the Liberal Democrats. And yes, I had the trappings of success – the fine car and the nice home. Mumbai and Rajasthan seemed a long way away though they were never forgotten. But I was worried. When there is no noise in the jungle and everything is quiet, you wonder where the tiger is.

On 14 November 1994 I left the factory early to attend a charity function at the Dorchester Hotel and my mobile rang. It was my brother. He said the factory at the Triangle Centre in Southall was on fire: the tiger had roared. Immediately at times like this you start thinking the worst. Has anyone died? Is this the end of my business? How can I possibly supply my customers? How could this have happened? For a second time in my life fire seemed certain to destroy everything I had worked so hard to build up. We had 250 people working there, and the first thing I asked was whether everyone was safe. Fortunately the people had all been evacuated from the building and were standing around outside in their protective factory clothing. I turned the car round, went home, got into my jeans and headed for the factory.

It was the longest drive of my life. Even before I reached the plant I could see the flames lighting up the night sky. As I approached along the Uxbridge Road it seemed clear that nothing could possibly be salvaged, and so it turned out. Everything was destroyed; there was not even a spoon left. There was nothing the fire service could have done to save the building, although the warehouse was intact. All the staff, who miraculously had escaped unscathed, were looking on in tears. This was not just some investment, it was their livelihoods; they had no second business like Royal Sweets to fall back on. My brother Akbar and my daughters, Zeenat and Zarmin, were distraught. My nephew, Nizar, my sister's son, who had joined the company at its inception, was also there and he was a great help to me. It was like a death in the family. The culmination of really a lifetime's preparation, education, experience and plain hard graft had gone in one night of horror. All that remained were ashes.

Curiously, I believe this was my finest hour. Publicly I was strong as I walked among the staff and tried to cheer them up. Only when I got home at about two in the morning did the reality of what had happened truly sink in. A business that was turning over some £15 million a year was now just a burned-out shell. I burst into tears.

When I went back to the site the next day many of the ladies who worked for me were there weeping. They clung on to me, but I told them not to worry. Instantly I seemed to know what was the right course of action. I promised them that all would be well, and that the factory would be rebuilt. To be honest I was not even sure how this was possible: I suppose that I was once again making the sort of promise I made to my mother when I was a little boy reassuring her that I, not yet a teenager, would take care of everything. Just as I knew, standing beside my father's body, that it was up to me, I knew, standing there before the smouldering ruins of my factory, watching the firemen damp down the remains, that somehow I would find an answer. I did what was expected of me. I put on a brave and optimistic face.

In reality I was not alone. I had tremendous resources at my disposal.

My mother had taught me integrity and honesty, and those principles now came to my aid; I had learned their business application from experience, and the first rule was hard work. I was not afraid of that, and now it was time to roll up my sleeves once again and forget the fine living and sumptuous receptions for a time. Last and by no means least, I am convinced that I had the spiritual support of my staff. Now, if you are not a religious person you can call it goodwill or moral encouragement, but however you choose to describe it I am certain it helped carry me through this crisis. Our greatest test isn't not falling, but getting up every time we fall. I suppose I could have retired but I was determined to fight back.

Not only did I have tremendous moral inspiration but I also had the practical help of countless friends. One simply called up and told me to build another factory and "don't worry about the noughts on the cheque". And among my friends I count my customers. I felt an obligation not to let them down but I had to come clean and admit that I was unable to fulfil my contract. The morning after the fire I sent my brother, Akbar, with Ashok Kaul, round to Sainsbury's, Waitrose and other customers to explain what had happened, although they knew because it had been all over the newspapers and on television. I called David Sainsbury personally, and my first words to him were: "I am sorry David. I have let you down." He simply said: "Don't worry. Tell me what you need." He told me not to disband my workforce because he would absorb them until I was up and running again and then he would give them back to me. Waitrose was the same, promising to stick by me until the factory was rebuilt. David Faulkner, the managing director, came to me and gave me a lot of comfort. This was the reward for the integrity and the honesty my mother had instilled in me. With such support, I knew I could save the business: all I had to do was work out how.

My auditors and legal advisers came to me and said that now I did not have an operational business I should disband the workforce, give them notice and save some money that way. I said to my chief accountant that we would do nothing of the sort. They had been loyal to me when I needed them to help me build the business, and I could not simply make them all redundant. Apart from anything else, I would soon be needing their help again. Such disloyalty on my part would have been unthinkable. I told him to keep paying the staff as if nothing had happened, even though the payroll was £80,000 a week.

I am a very practical man. I believe this sort of incident also brings opportunities and demonstrates the best in people. With friends, staff and customers like these, I had the self-confidence to rebuild. But we had many sleepless nights at the time, worrying and wondering whether in truth the business could be kept going. It is one thing to show bravado; delivering is a different matter.

I established a war council of directors and executives charged with the very simple task of keeping the company alive from one day to the next. There were days when it was touch and go, but I knew we would prevail even though there were temptations put in my path to take the easy option. While I was still looking for an alternative factory to start producing again, I was approached by a very large company who were also suppliers to my major customers. The managing director called me and asked to meet him in a café on the M4 motorway well away from Southall. I took with me my daughter, Zeenat, Ashok Kaul and my marketing agent. The MD made a stunning proposal to me. He said: "Your factory is destroyed – why don't you give me all your recipes of original Indian food? I will supply the chefs, staff and facilities and I will change the name of my company to Noon. In return I will pay you up-front money and a certain percentage of the profits for the next ten years, plus you can keep all the insurance money you get."

On something like this I react instantly and don't think about it very much. I put down my coffee cup and looked hard at the MD, who I could tell felt the terms were irresistible – which indeed they were from a purely financial perspective. I said it sounded like a fantastic offer, but could he please advise me. What would I tell my 250 people who escaped death in the fire, and came out into the cold in their factory clothes, and who shed tears with me in the night? What could I tell them? Just to go home? I will now be rich and the best of luck?

If you treat people like bits of property, you will soon get the same treatment back. The staff were just as much family to me as my own brothers and daughters. They had contributed to the success of the business as much as anyone, so it was unthinkable that I would take the money. I said I would not accept his offer, and instead I would rebuild my business. And I told him to make a note because I would now always be a thorn in his side. He said he didn't understand the Asian mentality. If he had made the same offer to an Englishman, it would have been accepted. I am not so certain about that. I don't think it is anything to do with culture, but is a question of character. Do you stand by those who have stood by you when trouble hit, or do you cut and run, grabbing the money when it is offered? What would I have said to David Sainsbury, or to David Faulkner at Waitrose, or to any of my other customers and friends who without hesitation had offered their help? Yes, of course, I am in business to make money, but as you know by now food is not just a business for me – it is a passion. So we said our goodbyes and I headed off back into London almost reinvigorated by the experience. I was more determined than ever to restore our production as quickly as possible. There was work to be done.

Within three weeks I knew we had turned the corner. It was a monumental team effort. When everyone is so determined to succeed it is practically impossible to fail, but that doesn't mean I wasn't worried. In fact we never actually stopped production altogether as we were able to make use of our own Bombay Halwa capacity, working in three shifts and cleaning up as we went along.

The only villains of the piece were the insurance companies who short-changed me and paid me peanuts against losses I suffered worth several millions. To begin with they did not want to pay me anything. I was stunned. I told them that I had enough credibility in the market to raise the money. I would beg, borrow or steal, I would mortgage my own house and my children's houses, but I would find the money. They could be sure that I would fight them all the way through the courts and they would end up paying me millions. Within eight days they came back to me and agreed to pay, but only a fraction of what I thought I was due.

Beware all growing businesses: I advise everyone to check their insurance cover every three months. If you are over insured, they won't pay you; if you are under insured, they won't pay you. Double-check with your own experts every comma and full stop on your policies because those terms will be thrown back at you when you put in a claim. Insurance, in my opinion, is a con game.

So I immediately started looking for a suitable factory that had extra capacity, where I could get back to work while my own factory was being rebuilt. David Sainsbury introduced me to the Hazelwood company, and out of the blue Peter Bar – subsequently Sir Peter Bar – called me and said he had heard what I had been through and that he had a company, Rowan Foods, which was part of the group, with a factory in Wrexham, North Wales, that I could use between 6 p.m. and 7 a.m. until I had rebuilt. I sent eight of my chefs and other staff up there and rented a house, and we salvaged our frozen food business.

This safety net was vital, because although major customers like Waitrose, Sainsbury's and Trust House Forte, which accounted for two thirds of our sales, had promised to keep our contracts alive, customers would soon go elsewhere. David Sainsbury had even gone so far as to keep his supermarket shelves empty for seventeen days until we could get production moving again, rather than go to a competitor. Some of the shelves even had notices informing customers about the fire and explaining why there were no products to buy. This was unprecedented loyalty and evidence of a belief in our ability to keep our promise to deliver.

In the meantime I spent £500,000 on new equipment and enlarged the Bombay Halwa plant for the chilled food that was the bigger part of our operation. Soon we were back to about 40 per cent of our original production. It may sound unlikely to those who do not believe in such things, but all along I know that my staff – Muslims, Sikh and Hindus – were praying for me in their temples, mosques and gurdwaras. Lo and behold, in less than two months I had found a property a few hundred yards from my old plant. It was 50,000 square feet and perfect, so I asked my agent to sort out the details. The building was owned by Metalbox, which is a large company, and I was worried that the details might take some time to be worked out. It so happened that I knew a senior board member of Metalbox, Ian Carmichael, but he was in Singapore. By chance his wife, Margaret, had an important position in Waitrose. I explained the situation to Ian on the phone and asked him if he would give me a good reference to his board back in London because I was in a terrible mess. By the time I called the man running the Metalbox office in Southall, the message had got through to him. I arranged a meeting and forty-five minutes later I emerged with a contract that could have otherwise taken months to secure. Again, the unwavering support of friends, this time at Waitrose, paid off.

I took over the plant in March 1995, employed a British company to fit it out, and on 13 August the Indian High Commissioner at the time, Dr L.M. Singhvi, opened the plant, which was almost double the size of the original. In no time at all the factory was filled to capacity. Fortunately, I found another plot in the same area and built another factory of about 45,000 square feet, and soon that too was working flat out.

On paper we had taken a hit, but life has a much bigger balance sheet and I look at what we really gained. If my customers before the fire were simply loyal, they had now become real friends. We also had a brand new factory with state-of-the-art equipment and the best fire safety system money could buy: divided sections with fire blankets, sprinkler systems with back-up pumps, alarm systems everywhere, and over each cooking pan its own fire suppression system – it transpired that the fire had been caused by an overheating pan.

Just to add insult to injury, as I was trying to get started again some people complained about smells from extractor fans at our premises and we were fined £14,000 by magistrates. I readily admitted it. The fans were installed according to the instructions of the environmental authorities and regularly updated, but my priority was to get back to business and provide work for my staff. I am sorry if it caused grief for our neighbours, but I learned my lesson and in the new factory I installed an odour control system that cost hundreds of thousands of pounds. Now you only notice the aroma when you are actually inside the buildings.

I was once asked what I thought was the key to my success, and after mentioning the importance of determination, luck and investing in new technology whenever possible, I concluded that the two most important factors were your customers and your staff. I believe it is vitally important to support your customers, even when they are finding life difficult. We reduce our prices without reducing quality if we believe that it will help our customers – in this case the supermarkets – to survive. Customer satisfaction is everything, whether you are making shoes or making curries. Equally important are your staff. Cut costs at every possible corner, but never scrimp and save on the wages. It may be one of your highest costs, but your staff are worth every penny. If you treat them as you would treat any member of your family, they will stand by you in times of crisis. Without them you are nothing.

Chapter Ten

THE NOON FOUNDATION, UNIONS AND FAMILY INVOLVEMENT

Once I was confident that Noon Products was firmly established and Bombay Halwa was secure, I began thinking about the future. You will not be surprised to know that I was not going to just sit back and reap the rewards of my hard work – or (lest I receive a spiritual slap from my mother for bragging) *our* hard work. There was still much more I could do in the UK; there were also markets in Europe, and there was the possibility of launching other menus – Chinese, Italian and even French. Why not? After all, we understood spices and flavouring.

Whenever you are flagging, in whatever enterprise or endeavour, there is nothing quite like a word of encouragement or a pat on the back to give you a boost. One of the highlights of the 1990s for me – certainly a terrific boost and a moment when I really thought I had arrived – was being made a Member of the Order of the British Empire (MBE), in the 1996 New Year's Honours list, for services to the food industry. We had come a long way since Noon Products plc had been formed just seven brief years earlier. Her Majesty the Queen, through her Conservative government under the premiership of John Major, had seen fit to recognise what we had done, but I in turn wanted to emphasise what Asians and their British hosts could do together. So I was delighted, just two weeks later, to be able to address the London Chamber of Commerce and Industry (LCCI) and stress the rich diversity of our two cultures and also show how together they could flourish.

This working together was a theme I would return to in the years that followed.

I was a co-founder and former chairman of the Asian Business Association, and we worked under the wing of the LCCI. Later, having been appointed to its board, I was honoured to be elected President of the LCCI in January 2002 by a unanimous vote – the first non-white to hold the post in its 120-year history. In one of my first speeches I would applaud the fact that London was a truly cosmopolitan city where immigrants had "infused fresh vitality into our institutions and invigorated our system". Large immigrant communities had brought a breath of fresh air to London.

Meanwhile, I was pulled back to reality when in November 1997 an industrial dispute over trade union rights began. I was reluctant to meet representatives of the GMB union as I felt I had a good working relationship with my staff – there was a sense of mutual loyalty. But the dispute over pay and the right to union representation grew protracted and acrimonious. At one stage, in January 1998, the protest brought production at the Collett Way facility to a halt while 200 staff staged a sit-in in the staff canteen. The following month staff joined a march and rally through the streets of Southall.

By now I was an open supporter of the Labour party. The new, youthful, Labour Prime Minister, Tony Blair, called me to his office and asked me why I was not recognising the unions. I told him that I would be happy to recognise them once the White Paper for the Fairness at Work Bill, giving workers the right to union representation if the majority of the staff were in favour, was presented to Parliament, but warned in jest that if there was union trouble I knew where he lived. Trouble of a different kind lay ahead for us both.

Finally, in August 1998, I agreed to sit down and talk about union representation and I eventually signed a deal in March 1999, witnessed by the GMB General Secretary, John Edmonds, recognising the union's right to bargain over pay and conditions. In the end the decision was up to the 400-strong workforce. We live in a democratic society, and 58 per cent of them decided that they wanted union representation. I was happy to accept.

But I had already begun thinking beyond the commercial sector. Perhaps it was time to start giving something back to a country that had welcomed me with open arms and allowed me to build my business, and whose people had supported and befriended me. The question was what should I do? There was no point in just making a donation here and a donation there to charity. My effort needed to be more focused and organised.

Outside work I was most concerned about education and healthcare so in 1995 I established my own charity, The Noon Foundation, which received an injection of £4 million in 2000. I decided to concentrate on these two areas (although I am always ready to support any worthwhile cause). A good education is by far the greatest gift we can give our children and after that we must take care of their health.

Why have a foundation? This was not a new idea. I had established a foundation in 1969 in Mumbai, and although I didn't have much money to donate then, we helped where we could, most notably in education. The money went direct to schools, to help distressed families in a form of scholarship. This assistance was not just for Muslim children but for anyone for whom I thought we could make a difference. Since I started the foundation we have helped thousands of boys and girls through their school and higher education at all levels. We even helped one Bangladeshi girl go to Harvard. We have also help educate quite a few students in the UK. You don't have to be a billionaire or even a millionaire, I believe: just give whatever you can, even if it is only to one person.

On one visit to India I saw the son of one of my servants in Bhawani Mandi playing near my home. I asked his father which school the boy was going to and it turned out to be the local municipal school. On the spur of the moment I offered to pay for him to go to a private school, and in order for him to catch up with the other pupils arranged for him to have some extra tuition. Sometimes I do these spontaneous things – but it is my money, and no one can complain. Similarly, I saw three or four children running round in the compound where we live. They were smart-looking kids, full of energy. I called them all over and said that I was leaving the next day and did not have time to talk to them then, but that the next time I was in India I would like to come to see them. On my return I arranged for them all to have private education. It will change their lives, and it gives me great pleasure to see them blossom.

Lack of education can be a great barrier. If you have it, it gives you great confidence, if you don't it can be a great handicap. If you educate one child, it is contagious. You cannot change the entire world – don't think about that – but if you can change one life, that is enough. I was delighted to help rebuild my old school in Sunel, now called the New Haideria English Secondary School, which is open to all pupils regardless of creed or race; it is flourishing with an enthusiastic staff and eager pupils studying every subject including those important for the future: environmental issues, computer technology and languages.

It is invidious to single out particular people or enterprises that we have been able to help over the years through the Noon Foundation, but I remember one of my happiest moments was when I was able to present a cheque for £100,000 to Norwich City Football Club's Youth Academy. The idea was for eight-to-eighteen-year-olds to be able to pursue their football dreams. The aim of the Academy was nothing less than to create the best facility of its kind in the country. Admittedly cricket is my game, but I am a sports fanatic, and there was another compelling reason why I wanted to help. The chairman of Norwich City Football Club was none other than Bob Cooper, the man who was prepared to take a risk and give me a chance when he was marketing director at Sainsbury's.

The Foundation also supported a mentoring programme to improve the career prospects of disadvantaged youngsters living in East London's Tower Hamlets by covenanting £200,000. I was fortunate as a young man to have people I could go to for advice and guidance, but what do you do if you have no one you can look up to or to whom you can turn? What do you do if you are always being turned down or having your ideas rejected as fanciful or farfetched just because of your postcode? What if you feel you have an artistic skill or a bright new business plan but there is no one with whom you can discuss it? The idea will simply die. This situation is precisely what the scheme run by Tower Hamlets College seeks to overcome. The college's very location is a mirror of the challenges these people face: 20 per cent of the workforce are unemployed and 35 per cent are from so-called ethnic minority backgrounds. (I loathe that expression, despite having been appointed by the UK's Department of Trade and Industry to the board of the Ethnic Minority Business Forum in February 2000 and serving for three years.) Right next door is the famous Square Mile of the City of London, one of the richest plots of land on the planet, and yet for many of these youngsters and potential entrepreneurs it might just as well be a thousand miles away.

The aim of the scheme is to provide youngsters over sixteen years of age with role models – successful people in the community who can share their experience and give practical first-hand advice about the skills and attitudes these young people will need to achieve their own goals in life. Too often they are frustrated in their ambitions because they lack the basic information, or maybe they just need a bit of a break in order to succeed. Some may simply not know how to conduct themselves at an interview. The mentoring scheme enables the college to develop training programmes and the support material that these youngsters will need, and mentors can meet them on a weekly basis.

I recall saying at the time that the scheme would help open doors for the students and give them a third-person view on the world. It is all very well having a bright idea, but in order to innovate you have to be able to turn those ideas into reality. I was asked who I would choose as a mentor and what qualities I would look for. I replied in Urdu "Bulund Khayal", which means a high-thinking visionary. My mother was my mentor. She taught me about what was important in life: integrity, honesty, tolerance and respect, and so much more. She was not educated in the traditional sense of the word but she built my foundations. Everyone needs a mentor, whether to encourage ambition or to gently guide youthful exuberance.

Among the projects supported by the Noon Foundation have been a production at the Royal Shakespeare Company, the Royal College of Organists, the Gujarat Earthquake Appeal and the Arpana Charitable Trust (helping the underprivileged in the rural areas of Karnal, near Delhi), as well as individuals such as the up-and-coming Jewish glass designer Adam Aaronson and other artists whom we have been able to assist.

Through the Noon Foundation, much later in 2007, we were able to support Birkbeck College, University of London, with a £200,000 donation in the form of bursaries to students over a four-year period. Birkbeck exemplifies precisely what I mean by the continuation of learning throughout life. The vast majority of its 19,000 plus students are part-timers finding opportunities after their normal work for further higher education. But it also provides an opportunity for people whom higher education at university may have passed by or for whom it may simply not have been regarded as relevant, particularly if they were women from minority groups. Birkbeck's immediate catchment area is East London, which has a high proportion of Muslim residents. Our aim was to help students who fell into the "poverty trap", earning enough to be above the threshold for government funding but not enough to support their studies.

I said in my opening remarks: "Islam is blamed for some of the worst ills of our times but we need to differentiate betwen the religion and its followers. Every religion has, and has had in the past, zealots and fanatics who have made life miserable for others. There is no excuse for them. But their religion is not to blame. At the heart of each world religon is enshrined the values of love, humility and charity. If ignorant and aggressive men have chosen to misinterpret the teachings and use them as an excuse for war, we can hardly blame religion for that. The core values of Islam are mercy, compassion and brotherhood." This is a theme I shall return to later.

Increasingly there is also a new group of students from Eastern Europe who are driven to improve themselves – many are single parents or even refugees. Under the energetic chairmanship of my friend Lord (Colin) Marshall, Birkbeck's ethos is to ensure that finance should not be a barrier to learning and that any student who wants to learn should not be prevented from doing so just because they do not have enough money.

One of my favourite charities is the Prince's Trust, established by HRH The Prince of Wales in 1976, and I am privileged to serve as a member of its Advisory Council. I first got involved with the Trust in the 1980s when I came back from America. I was very impressed with the work of the Trust to help young people overcome barriers and provide practical support, training, advice and financing to help them realise their ambitions. Since that time I have been able to meet Prince Charles on a number of occasions and I have supported the Trust whenever I could. The biggest event we were able to stage was in March 2003 when we organised a dinner for 350 people at the Dorchester Hotel. The Noon Foundation paid for the evening so when we sold a table for £10,000 the entire sum raised – about £212,000 – went to the Prince's Trust to allocate to any project it chose to support.

I discuss elsewhere the importance of trying to improve oneself without relying on state handouts later, but I am always ready to help those who help themselves. All the individuals I have been able to support either with my own money or formally through the Noon Foundation have been eager to get on in life. They were not taking my money because it was charity but because they recognised that this support would help them improve their lives and the lives of their families. They wanted to get on in the world and I recognise the same fire in the belly that I had as a young man.

★ ★ ★

I realise that anything I do through the Foundation is just a drop in the huge ocean of suffering. I often explain my action by telling the story of a young man sitting by the seashore. Each wave leaves behind it hoards of fish gasping for breath, and the young man picks up as many as he can and throws them back into the water. He cannot possibly keep up. A passer-by asks what he is doing as he seems to be wasting his time – there are so many fish that most of them will die before he can get to them. The passer-by asks what difference he thinks he is making. Undeterred, the young man picks up another fish and tosses it back into the water and watches it swim away. "It made a big difference to that one," he says.

Teaching and mentoring is all part of the wider learning process of getting along with each other regardless of background, and this is something I will look at more closely later on. By learning about and understanding one another we are more likely to appreciate our differences rather than squabble over them. It was with this process in mind that the Noon Foundation supported the British Library's technological initiative called Turning the Pages. Using virtual reality software and touch-screen technology, the public are able to "turn the pages" of precious texts. We arranged for the digitisation of Sultan Baybars' Qur'an, an Islamic treasure of the Mamluk period. This is a beautiful work in seven volumes that has survived since the fourteenth century.

Some years later, in May 2008, we were able to support an initiative to use the same technology for the exhibition The Ramayana: Love and Valour in India's Great Epic at the British Library. The Ramayana is an ancient Sanskrit epic poem attributed to the Hindu sage Valmiki, *c.* 400–200 BC, and has had a significant influence on Sanskrit poetry and Indian art and culture. It explores the importance of *dharma,* or duty and morality. At the heart of it is a great love story between Rama, the seventh incarnation of the god Vishnu, and his wife, Sita. *Rama ayana* literally means "Rama's journey". Now for the first time scholars are able to study many of the exquisite illustrations from the seventeenth-century manuscript, which was commissioned by Rana Jagat Singh of Mewar. So it was appropriate that the present head of that great dynasty, Shriji Arvind Singh Mewar, His Highness the Maharana of Udaipur, allowed me to persuade him formally to inaugurate the exhibition in London. In his speech His Highness spoke of the importance of making such stories available to a wider audience in order to improve understanding between peoples. And in the same spirit of increasing knowledge and understanding the Noon Foundation gave £500,000 to the Oxford Centre for Islamic Studies in August 2008.

Sometimes it is important for people to remember the sacrifice of others on their behalf. So the Foundation supported a project to build the Memorial Gates in Hyde Park, which was a Millennium project to mark the contribution of Indian soldiers during the two World Wars. The Gates are situated on Constitution Hill in London and were officially inaugurated by Her Majesty the Queen on 6 November 2002. The success of this particular project was in no small part thanks to the inspiration and drive of Baroness Flather, JP, DL, Patron of the Memorial Gates Trust, whose father, Aftab Rai, served in the First World War in Mesopotamia where 29,555 members of the Indian Army died.

Even now, as I prepare these words in my seventies, I still feel I have so much more to do. I was immensely honoured to be awarded the Asian Business Network's Outstanding Lifetime Achievement Award, kindly presented by the Rt Hon. Jack Straw MP, what now seems a long time ago in 1998, but my lifetime was not over and there will always be more that I want to achieve. For example, I would like to do more construction back in my home town of Bhawani Mandi and in Sunel where the need is great. I have been building my hospital there and have also created a hall for the unfortunate dalits and contributed to an irrigation system with a mini dam to improve the water supply and sanitation conditions for ten villages. No one has pressurised me to do these things; they give me great pleasure and I shall continue to do them as long as I am able. After all, my father and his brother built two hospitals when they did not have much money. If you like, I am just following a family tradition.

* * *

But I am getting ahead of myself and there were important developments to be accomplished at work before the new Millennium dawned. Although I was the titular head of Noon Products and Bombay Halwa, I always wanted the family to be involved as it had been since I was a boy. The business in India was being run by my eldest brother, Abbas, supported by immediate members of his family. Back in London my younger brother, Akbar, was my deputy at Noon Products. He was brilliant in all aspects of buying and had excellent management skills. When you are a family business everyone has to do a bit of everything: he even drove fork lift trucks when necessary and I worked in the packaging department on Saturdays.

I was thrilled that my daughters, Zeenat and Zarmin, also wanted to be involved. Zarmin took on responsibility for launching and managing our Noon Taste of India Restaurant at Heathrow's Terminal One – the first Indian restaurant in a European Airport. It was opened on 28 October 1996 in response to the passengers' desire for a wider range of ethnic foods. They could get their fish and chips but it seems that what the British public also wanted just before they flew "abroad" was a good honest curry – and now they could get that sixteen hours a day, seven days a week, with everything prepared on site. After all, airlines were increasingly cutting down on what passengers could get in-flight. Our menu was specially designed by Ashok Kaul, our executive chef, and included some of the milder curries as well as providing things to go with an early morning coffee such as *idli sambar* (steamed fluffy rice and lentil cakes) or *medu wada sambar* (a sort of lentil dumpling.) Anyone concerned about eating a curry before flying in turbulent weather could be reassured because according to the Aviation Health Institute the spiciness of the food settles the stomach more quickly if the plane hits rough weather!

Even Egon Ronay, the revered and feared food critic, was quoted at the time as saying: "Curry is the national dish. It's the new sausages and mash. There has always been a soft spot for curry with the British." He added: "It's about time. This reflects the variety of restaurants that are available in London. I have tasted food at Mr Noon's factory and it was very good." In his first report ranking airport catering he described our restaurant as the most outstanding establishment at a UK airport and praised the "outstanding and exciting Indian cooking, innovative regional dishes and unobtrusive service". As I saw it, a high proportion of Europeans travelled through Terminal One so our restaurant was ideally placed to export the message of Indian cuisine in the UK to mainland Europe. It raised our company profile although it was not a profitable venture.

My elder daughter, Zeenat, was the highly competent operations director of Noon Products. She was trained by the Taj Group of Hotels as Food and Beverage Manager, working her way up from cutting vegetables in the kitchens to managerial level, and then when we started Noon Products she came over to us. In short, we have all done everything in the business, from cleaning to preparation and cooking. In life, when the opportunity comes by you have got to grab it with both hands. If that means driving a forklift or working in the kitchen, so be it.

In the meantime our success had begun to attract attention. Our business was too big to be ignored by the much larger food manufacturers and was beginning to get too big for us to run like a small family outfit. At this stage we were turning over about £40 million. I knew in my heart of hearts that if I were run over by a bus the family would be in difficulty because the business depended on my skill as a manager, but much more importantly, on my credibility in the market to borrow money. We had borrowings of almost £9 million. So one thought constantly troubled me: if I died, my children might say their father was a foolish man – he had created such a big circus and now they could not control the animals. Various suitors approached us and I decided that the time was right for change.

Chapter Eleven

Changes at Noon Products

M y main concern about giving up control of my "baby"– and there is
always something of parental concern about a business you have
built from scratch – was to find a buyer who would continue with the same
ethos of quality and authenticity that we had nurtured. On the table was
Noon Products Ltd; I never wanted to give up the core, original sweet
operation of Bombay Halwa Limited. Money was not the prime motivation. I was not prepared to sell out just for the highest offer, because I wanted
continuity of the Noon brand and the standards my staff and I had pursued.

I was approached by a medium-sized publicly quoted firm called WT
Foods Ltd. They were distributors and not experienced in manufacturing.
I knew them slightly by reputation and was confident that they would be
able to maintain the distinctive style of our operation; indeed they had no
wish to change anything about our approach. So then it came down to
money.

How do you evaluate your company? Normally a company is valued on
its EBITA, which indicates earnings before the deduction of interest, tax,
depreciation and amortisation, and then you multiply by a figure. Our
valuation on that basis would make the company worth £35 million.

At that stage I hadn't mentioned my plan to anyone in the family apart
from my brother Akbar, and I had also told my auditor, Jahangir Mehta,

whom I had taken into my confidence. They both thought this was the right price, and so did my lawyer, who of course had to be consulted. But I told them that they had all missed the point. It was not the right price. Noon had a brand value and I said I intended to hold out for £15 million for the brand alone; otherwise I was not prepared to sell. They thought it sounded a bit rich, but they knew better than to argue with me once my mind was made up.

We had three meetings with WT Foods but it was stalemate; they wanted to buy and I wanted to sell but neither of us would budge from our positions. Finally my brother and I and the chief executive and finance director of WT Foods met for lunch at Mosimann's, one of London's fashionable restaurants. I was not prepared to back down from the £50 million, plus I wanted them to pay all my debt of nearly £9 million. Then I had one of those moments of serendipity that occasionally happen in life. Quite by chance the actress Susan Hampshire, who launched a new range of Indian meals for Noon Products in December 1994, was also dining at the restaurant. She saw me, walked over and she gave me a hug and a kiss on the cheek. Moments later Anton Mosimann, who was a friend, came out of his kitchen and shook hands with me. So I said to the WT people, who were most impressed, "You see, this is part of your brand. If Anton Mosimann knows Gulam Noon is eating in his restaurant he wants to come out of the kitchen and shake his hand. It is part of the brand and has a value. If an English actress comes and kisses you, it is your brand." The deal was clinched. It was to be a classic reverse merger under Stock Exchange rules, with WT Foods increasing its share capital by nearly 90 per cent to finance the transaction. Noon Products was bigger than WT Foods.

The moral of the story is when you are selling your business find out what your hidden strengths are – not only how much your turnover is or how many assets you have or how much is in your bank account, but what your brand leverage is. In my case the Noon Products name had become synonymous with quality. But again I would not cut and run. I said I would work for them for one year without a salary to ensure that we delivered on our promises. I also allowed them to keep £5 million in claw-back for a year until I had achieved the targets agreed within a two-year timeframe.

Right up to October 1998, the family were still not aware of the deal. They knew I had been considering floating the business on the Stock Exchange but as far as they were concerned at that stage it was just another option. Only when the price was fixed and the die was cast did I tell them all one morning in the office. To put it mildly, they were upset. In fact the reaction was pretty hostile. Asian family businesses were never sold: they were passed from one generation to the next. At the family "council of war", my daughter, Zeenat, was shocked. Her sister, Zarmin, was dumbfounded. Why had I done it, she asked. It was suggested in some quarters that the atmosphere in the business had changed with the union struggle, but that was not the rationale. I was simply doing what I believed was right for the family and they knew that there could be no going back. I had made my decision and they were not going to make me change my mind. As I think I have made clear, I can be a little stubborn.

When I explained the ramifications of possibly lumbering them with nearly £9 million of debt and that I was in fact selling the business to protect them, they understood. We had around 500 employees at that stage, a fantastic customer base and a good turnover, but to take this further we had to have more professionalism, more people and more finance. I warned them that the bank would not recognise them as an operator in the market. My daughters are capable, but not that capable of taking the risks I took and moving the business on. They are not me, and the same dynamism is not there. We cannot all be alike. Of course they quickly recognised the sense of what I was doing. I said in any case, why shouldn't we enjoy the money? I wanted to buy them each a house, pay off any mortgages and take care of our extended family in India.

I mentioned earlier the importance of succession in a family business, and I was taking my own advice. That is why I sold Noon Products. If something had happened to me, the children would have cursed me. They would say that they had been left with a monster that they could not control. One newspaper said I had "jettisoned an article of faith" of our community by selling the family business, but I have never seen the business like that. Yes, it was a family affair, but it was not run to keep the family occupied: it was run on commercial lines, with family members all earning their keep through sheer hard work and ability. And in any case, what had really changed? My role remained much as before. As part of the deal I stayed on as chairman and managing director of Noon Products and non-executive director of WT Foods. I was still effectively taking all the decisions about Noon Products although I was now answerable to my shareholders, and we had kept the Heathrow Restaurant out of the deal. The only difference was that we now did not have personal liability to the banks for a large loan: win–win, as they say.

In short, I think it was a fantastic decision and I pat myself on the back for taking it. When the deal hit the newspapers on 17 December 1998, the headlines read "Noon Got Full Value". Every analyst must have worked out the price and reached £35 million, and yet I got £50 million at a time when overall the food share market was down. It was also a good deal for WT Foods, which as Keith Stott, chief executive of WT, said at the time was "driven by synergy". WT already had interests in Indian, Oriental and Caribbean foods and Noon Products could benefit from WT's distribution networks in Southern Europe. In fact the proof was in the pudding. We built up the business to £60 to 70 million. The only strain was on the capacity of my two factories, which were bursting at the seams.

But I was tired of building a new factory every time we expanded, and I resolved to build a really large plant once and for all. So much for putting my feet up and enjoying the spoils of the WT deal! I was sixty-five years old and perfectly entitled to ease off the pressure, but I am not the sort of person who is prepared to sit back and live off interest.

Not only was life hectic on the business front. I had met and fallen in love with Mohini Kent, the film-maker, author and playwright, and we married in 1998 in a simple ceremony in a register office in London just a few weeks after I asked her to be my wife. Among her work, Mohini had scripted and directed a documentary called *Curry Tiffin*, a study of Indian history through the culinary traditions of the Hindus, Muslims and the British in India, so we certainly had an interest in food in common. She also wrote the narrative for *The Noon Book of Authentic Indian Cooking*, published by Harper Collins.

My search for a new factory site could not have been easier. There was another plot of five acres available on the same estate very close to my two factories. I leased it, got my technical team to draw up a state-of-the-art design and started work. It was going to be a major undertaking for which I needed at least £15 million. But because the market was still down it was thought unlikely that the shareholders would support such borrowing so we had to raise the finance a different way.

WT Foods was too small to raise funds in the city so in 2001, with the support of the venture capital firm Bridgepoint Capital, we bought back the entire group from WT Foods. I have to say that I was somewhat hesitant about going with a venture capital firm, but my reservations were unfounded. Bridgepoint were constructive and open-minded. By now WT Foods had eight companies, of which Noon Products was the jewel in the crown. It was de-listed in a deal worth over £100 million. Bridgepoint immediately injected millions towards the cost of the factory, which had the very latest technology that £15 million could buy. The facility was 147,000 square feet on a five-acre site and the only one in UK with Microban walls and floors to prevent the spread of germs. It could produce 1.5 million meals a week and this meant that we were now employing 1000 people. Soon afterwards we expanded our repertoire with the acquisition of Marston Valley Foods, who were specialists in Thai food as well as Indian cuisine.

I was absolutely thrilled when HRH Prince Charles, who had presented me with my MBE at Buckingham Palace, agreed to perform the formal opening ceremony two years later on a very warm 13 June 2003. I hope he enjoyed the comparison I noted between our output using sixty-eight different recipes and that of Queen Victoria's chef who published this recipe for curry in 1840: "Take two tablespoons of meat curry paste, one tablespoon of curry powder and add as much flour as required to thicken the sauce." I like to think Queen Victoria would have enjoyed our more adventurous dishes such as chicken tikka masala and coriander naan. One journalist was bold enough to predict that when Prince Charles was crowned king, curry would be served at the coronation banquet.

I have always been fortunate to enjoy the backing of a core of loyal staff throughout my business career, and now as a British citizen I have also always had the backing and recognition of the UK. Great Britain welcomed me, as they did so many of my countrymen, and I knew I would want to repay that kindness. In the midst of all our expansion, the ultimate accolade was conferred on me in 2002 when I was knighted by Her Majesty the Queen. That was a genuine surprise. I had no idea that my name would appear in the Honours List as the preliminary letter from Downing Street sent some weeks earlier had somehow been mislaid and they had to phone me to make sure I would accept. Not surprisingly I said yes! I was told not to say a word about it until the formal announcement was made, but naturally I could not keep something like that from my family. I telephoned Mohini to give this good news and called my daughters, who were in tears of delight, but I remember telling them that we must all keep our feet on the ground and not become arrogant just because of the great honour.

This was the Golden Jubilee Year of Her Majesty's reign, and during the year she visited every borough in the capital. Although I had been "gazetted" as receiving a knighthood I still had not been to Buckingham Palace for the investiture, but according to protocol I was from that moment known as Sir Gulam Noon. Now it so happened that the Queen was visiting Ealing on her tour. I was invited to the lunch by the Mayor of Ealing, Councillor Kieron Gavan, and I found myself sitting next to her. The Queen asked me, "Sir Gulam, what do you do?" and "Sir Gulam, how many people do you employ?" and "Sir Gulam, when did you come to this country?" and "Sir Gulam this and Sir Gulam that." So out of great respect and politeness I said, "Your Majesty, just Gulam will do." She looked straight into my eyes and said, "Sir Gulam, we give these titles, so I think we had better use them." She is such a fine human being that she is always able to put people who are nervous in her company at their ease and she said: "I won't be able to do the investiture. Charles will do it, but I will tell him to be careful of your ears with his sword." As it turned out her schedule must have changed and in fact she did knight me.

While we were having lunch, there was suddenly a great crash when a bucket of ice fell and all the ice cubes scattered under our table and over our feet. I apologised profusely, but all Her Majesty said was: "We do it all the time at home." Such a spontaneous remark – and she immediately settled all our jangling nerves.

Back in the business world the ever restless Bridgepoint, typical of any venture capital partner, were on the lookout for ways of getting a return on their investment. Actually that never concerned me at all. I remember saying to a journalist when rumours abounded about the future of the business because we were receiving numerous unsolicited offers that I was much more concerned about retiring than about someone buying us out. I am not a gardener or a carpenter and I am a hopeless handyman so I cannot imagine myself taking life easy. I like to be up and out of the house by 8.30 a.m., and 11.00 a.m. on Saturdays – I am always busy.

It is never the right time to step away from the daily battle of running a business, but it was now time to hand over the management to someone younger and more energetic. In late 2003 I was delighted to welcome John Duffy, first as operations manager and then as managing director while I became non-executive chairman. John was formerly operations director for Golden Wonder Holdings Limited and came to Noon Products from the WT Food Group. He was a good operator. He had his own style, and I was not getting any younger. It was time for some fresh blood.

If I am honest, I do not miss the sheer hard graft of the earlier days (although I keep my eye on the ball and still go to the factory every day around lunchtime after attending to my other business interests and will often stay until early evening). But there was still some important business for me to guide through, if not actually mastermind myself. The decision had been taken to break up WT Foods. It was inevitable once we had joined forces with a VC firm, and we were now growing rapidly. WT appointed Stamford Partners, a corporate finance boutique, to evaluate the offers we had been receiving. By July 2005 the field had been reduced to five possibles, including trade and equity bidders. Finally, after a relatively brief courtship, in August 2005 Noon Products was sold to Kerry Foods Limited of Ireland, a division of Kerry Group plc, for £124 million.

While negotiating with Kerry I was certain in my mind that I had to sell to someone who could maintain the culture of the organisation and take it forward. But more than that, I wanted to sell Noon Products into a company where it would remain and where our creation and our business ethos would be nurtured. There were many other bids from other venture capital firms and other food companies, but I was always keen on Kerry Foods. I knew the former CEO of Kerry Foods, Michael Griffith, and my brother and I used to meet him over the years. He used to come to the office even before we sold the business for the first time to WT Foods. But when I met Kerry Food's CEO, Flor Healy, and we spoke for forty-five minutes, I became convinced. He and I had been "locked in a room" alone together, and by the end I could say to myself: "Here is a man of commitment who is trustworthy." I recommended to my partner, Bridgepoint, that Kerry Foods was the right company.

If for some reason they had not wanted to go ahead, I think I would have distanced myself from the deal because I was certain I did not want the business to be passed on to yet another investment company. The venture capitalists' job was done. They had suited me at the time – they had funded me, they had done their job and enhanced our value – but to sell to another VC outfit was not on, and I would not have been party to it. to sell to a food company without our sense of quality would not have worked either, but in Flor Healey I found a man I could trust. He said: "I will not change your character, I will not change the ethos or culture of the comapny, I will not change anything." And he kept his word.

Once again I was invited to remain as a non-executive chairman to perform the ambassadorial role. My present managing director and great administrator and motivator is Bob Carnel. Turnover increased and my job was to hobnob at the senior and political levels. I have a skill at interacting with people. My face was well known and I also knew the staff, and continuity was important. They needed to see that it was business as usual. I still go round the factory, where we have a predominantly Asian workforce. There was definitely uncertainty for them as the business seemed to be going backwards and forwards between different owners: first there was WT, then Bridgepoint and now Kerry Foods. I provided a sort of moral and ethical stability.

The important point for Noon Products was that it now had a bigger and stronger parent to carry it forward. Kerry Foods had grown from a former milk co-operative in the 1970s into a global food group with annual sales of 4 billion Euro and employing some 20,000 people. The company is best known for brands such as Kerrymaid butter, Walls sausages, cheese strings and Mattessons meats. As far as Kerry Foods was concerned, Noon Products was a good fit with its own ready-made meals business, Rye Valley Foods, and it could now take a larger slice of the UK chilled ready-made foods market, then worth around £1.4 billion. At that time in 2005 Noon Products Ltd was employing 1000 people, and had a healthy pre-tax profit in 2004/5 on an equally healthy turnover. We were producing a quarter of million curries a day from more than 200 different recipes, of which chicken tikka masala is still the most popular.

The timing of the sale was right because the smaller operators were being squeezed by the competition and by price wars. The only way they could survive was through consolidation or by joining larger companies like Kerry that could provide them with additional resources and wider market exposure. I was content that the business was in safe hands.

Chapter Twelve

New Ventures

The very same day that we announced the sale of Noon Products to the Kerry Group, the papers picked up on the news that I had decided to back the takeover of one of Britain's leading manufacturers of natural and herbal remedies, the Birmingham-based company BioCare. I was not about to put on my carpet slippers just yet. While there is still breath in my body I will always be ready to listen to new ideas, and they don't have to be food based! In my book a deal is a deal; it is either a good one or a bad one. Yes, I am known for my food business and to some extent for the work I do through the Noon Foundation, but essentially every business proposition is the same. I am attracted to particular sectors (and I shall come to those), but I have friends in every walk of life. From time to time they suggest that we might co-operate in a joint venture and usually, because of the way my mind works, we have a go.

The BioCare deal was done through a cash shell called Neutrahealth. I put in some money. Members of the family also invested, and the remaining directors of Neutrahealth put in substantial capital. Other investors made up the balance. I had already taken a stake in the company, which was established that same year specifically to buy businesses in the natural healthcare sector.

The nutraceutical sector is all about organic food, products like yogurt and cereal bars, vitamins and alternative health products such as aromatherapy oils. It is a fragmented industry and our strategy is to consolidate it as a big package under one company and – who knows? – probably sell it. Neutrahealth has subsequently bought four or five companies and I am a solid backer of the venture. While I have always had an interest in health – I was a founder member of Cancer Research UK – the concept had also to make commercial sense. I am happy to say that shares picked up and we seem to be on our way. Overall, the market turned over £2.5 billion in 2006. As one headline put it, it is where food meets science. That sounds good to me. Neutrahealth has a young and energetic CEO, Michael Toxvaerd and financial director Robin Hilton. Between them they have done a sterling job for the company.

As I have mentioned, I am not one to live on interest payments alone and I get restless for new ventures. One day perhaps that fire in the belly will go out, but I doubt it. For example, I bought a call centre business in India in 2005 and sold it in 2007 for a good profit. Remembering my basic training as a young lad in reading a balance sheet, I will explore any idea as long as the numbers add up – although I would not buy a brewery! One of the biggest ventures to attract me was the booming property market. This was an interest I had not been able to indulge since as a precocious young man of twenty-something I had started buying property in Mumbai for all the family and as an investment.

I decided it was not appropriate for me to run my other business interests out of the Noon Products offices and I instructed agents to find me something suitable in central London where I could base my own Noon Group of companies. The agent found three properties for us to look at and the first was what would become my new base at Queen Anne's Gate. It was in a terrible condition. But I liked the location right opposite St James's Park; on one side is Buckingham Palace and on the other, the Houses of Parliament. I said: "This is the place." The agent wanted me to look over the other two buildings, but I assured him that I was not going to change my mind. I asked what the price was and agreed to pay it in full. I was not interested in haggling. I am not pretending to be an expert, but my instincts about the building proved right sooner than I had expected. We completed very quickly and two weeks later my solicitor received a call from the vendor's solicitor asking if I was interested in becoming £500,000 richer by selling the property back. My answer was short and not so sweet. I needed an office and set about carrying out the refurbishment.

My daughters and my brother came to have a look at what I had bought and they were unanimous in their opinion: "You are mad. It is in a filthy condition. It is a Grade I property and the authorities will make your life miserable." To top it all, I got a visit from English Heritage who asked if I realised that it was a listed building and that there were certain rules and regulations about what could be done with the refurbishment. I told the man from EH not to worry as I had found an architect who had worked on Windsor Castle after the fire in November 1992, Donald Insall. That seemed to satisfy him. I used to go round to the building every morning at eight o'clock because I wanted to stamp my personality on every room, and on every panel.

The "mad investment" seems to have worked out quite well. Now with a consortium of friends led by Shabir Randeree, we buy other properties, usually in central London and happily have done well. Shabir and his father, Ahmedbhai Randeree, are the epitome of integrity and I work closely with their company, DCD.

However, as I am no longer quite so tied to the day-to-day affairs of Noon Products I find myself travelling more than ever. During the first part of the new millennium it seemed that wherever one turned property prices were rising, and one of my biggest ventures was in Bahrain with my good friend Mohammed Dadabhai. Happily, there is a family connection as my sister's grandson, Aziz, married Mohammed's daughter, Fatima. Like me, Mohammed has been a businessman since his childhood. His father, Shaikh Ahmed Ali Dadabhai, arrived in Bahrain in 1935 and had a humble start to his working life. He ran a toyshop, and Mohammed would hurry back from school to learn his trade: the story may sound familiar! Mohammed takes great pride in remembering that he used to sell toys as a hawker on the street corners. But he quickly assumed responsibility for the family business, which he diversified into different sectors including hotels and luxury property.

I became a partner with Mohammed in three hotels, investing several million dollars. We built and sold a five-star hotel and through him I met the King of Bahrain, His Majesty Shaikh Hamad Bin Isa Al Khalifa, the Prime Minister, His Highness Sheikh Khalifa Bin Salman Al Khalifa, and all the business leaders there. Above all, our aim was to expose Bahrain to the Asian community and to the Asian markets, both in the UK and in India. In 2006 there were reported to be about 350,000 people of Indian and Pakistani origin living in Bahrain – the largest population group after indigenous Bahrainis.

While the Asian community has undoubtedly being doing well in several parts of the Middle East, including in Bahrain where many have adopted Bahraini citizenship, there are tensions with the local population feeling squeezed by the presence of so many Asians. But just as in Britain I know that we have made a significant contribution at all levels in commerce and society in general, so too in Bahrain I believe our community has been able to fill a gap in the market. By providing services and creating new industries, and with those industries new jobs, I am convinced that we can enhance any society in which we live. It matters not a jot in my book when Asians adopt Bahraini or British citizenship, as that simply establishes a closer bond with the country in which they have chosen to live. In my book they then cease to be an ethnic minority – a dreadful phrase – and become full citizens of the country, working with the tools at their disposal. Bahrain is famous for its gold, so that is another area where Mohammed Dadabhai and I have made an effort. In 2000 he opened what was dubbed a "gold city" with 120 shops selling only gold products. What Asians are doing in whatever land we find ourselves is celebrating what that land has to offer – working with its resources, its culture and its people. In the end it comes down to understanding and learning about one another, and this spirit of learning and education is one of my great passions.

I have been privileged to be involved in a number of government-backed business initiatives in Bahrain, including the International Conference for Organisational Development inaugurated by the Prime Minister, Sheikh Khalifa Bin Salman Al Khalifa, and attended by many international figures including the former US President George Bush senior. This is all part of the process of sharing and understanding in business and politics. His

Majesty Sheikh Hamad Bin Isa Al Khalifa and the Crown Prince, Shaikh Salman Bin Hamad Al-Khalifa, have always made visiting delegations extremely welcome – it is not in every country that I visit that I am given an escort of police outriders. While that may do wonders for my ego, the real message is that Bahrain and its leaders value new business and are open to all comers. It is only by people from different backgrounds and experiences meeting in this way that real understanding develops between nations, as exemplified by Dr Hassan Fakhro the Commerce Minster, who has done a great job for his country.

I have travelled widely in the region and I find Bahrain to be a very educated, pluralistic society, and liberal for a Muslim country. It allows synagogues, churches and Hindu temples, and they even have a Jewish lady in their Shura or Parliament, which illustrates their attitude. In fact Mohammed Dadabhai was also appointed to the Shura, so even "outsiders" can earn important positions within the country. I am a teetotaller and don't smoke, but having lived in a very open and moderate society like Britain I don't like to be told what I can and cannot do. Nobody there says you can't drink this or you can't eat that. I was surprised to find that the Christian community can even buy pork and liquor in Bahrain. If you don't want to eat pork, that's fine, but they are happy for people who do want to eat it to be allowed to buy what they want.

This is a very important point for businesses. Any country that imposes artificial restrictions will create a barrier for business entry. In India it happened for a long, long time until the government eased the exchange control system. There is still much to be done. The analogy used is that India is like a Formula One car being driven with the brake on. I am not critical – no society is perfect – but every country has to realise that the world is a village. We live in a global economy. You cannot have a small-frog-in-a-well mentality: you must come out and see what is going on around you. I am very happy to say that the Asian community has responded to this challenge and is now spread all over the world. Asians are generating wealth not only for their families but for the countries in which they live.

Sometimes one can be of service to India as a result of one's good fortune in the UK. A sudden call for help back in 1998 was just such an occasion. A package of letters and cards in English and in Urdu, written by Mahatma Gandhi – some in his own hand – to the Muslim leader, Maulana Abdul Bari, between 1918 and 1924 had been put up for sale at Sotheby's. They were part of a package of literature including correspondence by Pandit Jawaharlal Nehru and his father, Motilal Nehru, and there was a real danger that the letters might be lost into private hands. The former Indian High Commissioner, Dr L.M. Singhvi, who had opened my new plant after the big fire in 1995 but by now, three years later, was back in Delhi and a Rajya Sabha MP, called me to see whether I could help. These were important documents running to thirty-eight pages of text detailing Gandhi's thoughts on Hindu-Muslim unity and the concept of making secularism the main plank of the Indian freedom movement.

I would like to quote from his letter written from Sabarmati on 2nd March 1922 to Maulana Saheb:

> "*That our opponents have magnified our violence and terrorised us is only too true, but we expected no more from them and no less. Hindus are as bad as Musselamans., but unfortunately as both are weak our policy depends for its success upon the hearty co-operation of both, and I have no doubt this non-violence as a policy merely will never succeed if it is followed only by one party, and it may be that God wishes to punish us so thoroughly for our weakness that he will not set our hearts working towards non-violence. I see quite clearly that we have not fully succeeded only because we have not been fully non-violent.*"

He went on: "*What is now to be done is the question. I am clear that all aggressive activity must be stopped. Our ranks must be weeded of all undesirable elements. If really as a result of our experiment we have come to the conclusion that it is impossible to control the mass violence or to convince the majority of our countrymen of the necessity of remaining non-violent we may revise our programme, but it would be suicidal to delude ourselves into the belief that we are following the policy of non-violence when we are not. I can see my way clear to working out our way even with a staunch minority.*

> "*Please think over the matter and let me know what can be done.*

If we can re-establish a non-violent atmosphere we must be able to work out the constructive programme laid down. It will be a test of our sincerity and it will give strength to us which we cannot gain by any other means."

When it came to the auction, Dr Singhvi was determined to save the letters for Indian posterity and was sure the money would be raised one way or another from private funds. A lawyer representing him did the bidding. In the end, my close friend Nat Puri, the successful Nottingham-based businessman, and I covered the final price between us. It is moments like this that make all the work one has done worthwhile. Dr Singhvi said at the time: "It is symbolic that the letters were bought jointly by a Muslim and a Hindu." And he was right when he said: "It was essential to get these rare papers back as they are a part of our national heritage." The letters are now the property of the Indian government.

It was not the first time I had been able to save valuable documents of Mahatma Gandhi for India. Five years earlier, my friend Lord Raj Bagri and I, in partnership, successfully bid at auction for a collection of the Mahatma's hand-written letters and returned them to the Indian government.

I sit on numerous advisory boards, offering guidance where I can, and more often than not these boards are related to social projects. For example, I am on the advisory board of Bridges Ventures, the venture capital firm founded by Sir Ronald Cohen, which seeks to invest in socially beneficial projects in deprived areas of the UK. There are quite a number of leading financial figures all doing what they can, including Philip Yea, chief executive of 3i, the listed private equity group, Chai Patel of Priory Healthcare, and Tom Singh, the founder and non-executive director of New Look, the clothes retailer, who together with Sir Ronald co-founded Bridges. Bridges has raised £75 million from the private sector to invest in its projects. It is a commercial venture as well, and the intention, as with all VC businesses, is to see a good return for investors. It is possible to do good in the world and still make a profit. Bridges is now going from strength to strength.

Ever eager to learn and now with time to explore new avenues, I am always prepared to make a contribution if it seems worthwhile. I believe that one should be involved if one can in public services and public bodies. There is no money in it, but my point is that I can learn and interact with people and make new friends. I was invited by the Conservative government of the day onto the Covent Garden Market Authority and appointed by an Act of Parliament. Covent Garden is the largest fresh fruit and vegetable market in the country owned by the UK government. I was appointed because they felt they needed more commercial experience, more business sense. Most people were on the board for one or two years but my appointment kept being renewed until after six years in 2001 I eventually decided that I should make room for someone younger.

One of the most demanding positions I have held, and one concerned with a subject that must be dear to the heart of anyone who has had to tackle London's traffic, was serving on the board of TfL (Transport for London), which I joined in 2004. Ken Livingstone, then London's Mayor, phoned me when I was in a British Airways lounge waiting for a flight to Mumbai and asked if I was prepared to join.

In politics, sometimes you win and sometimes you lose, and Ken Livingstone received praise and condemnation in equal measure while he was Mayor of London. What I would say is that he is probably the most hard-working man I have ever met. You may not agree with all his ideas, but he is a very committed man. Of course, this was not enough to convince the people of London to re-elect him and on 3 May 2008 Livingstone was defeated in the London Mayoral election by the Conservative candidate, Boris Johnson.

Strictly in terms of getting London moving, I personally would advocate more tunnels or flyovers because the traffic is a nightmare for cars in the inner city. Forget the circular roads like the M25, which is now full: the focus has to be on moving traffic across London because drivers today have to fight for every inch. In Mumbai we have a three-kilometre flyover in the middle of the city that passes through the area where I used to live. It was terribly congested but now it is much better. Even in comparatively smaller cities like Hyderabad or Jaipur there are flyovers, but of course there they are starting with a blank sheet of paper while London has to build around years of infrastructure. These are ambitious ideas, but for a situation like the present one you need to make ambitious plans. Ideally, of course, there would be a public transport system that would persuade people to leave their cars at home, but a great deal needs to be done before that will happen.

The problem is that London seems to have become the centre of the universe, and its roads cannot cope. There needs to be a proper coordinated transport system. For thirty or forty years it has been largely neglected, and just patched up when something breaks. Millions if not billions of pounds need to be invested to improve services. Gradually this is being done – the tube system is being modernised and the bus services improved – but I do not suppose that there is a single commuter who has a good word to say about the journey to and from work every day. It will be interesting to see how London copes with the 2012 Olympic Games and the influx of millions of spectators and Olympic squads. Crowds are the price you pay for success. London fights hard and well to maintain its reputation as the financial centre of the world, just as it fought hard and well to win the bid for the 2012 Games. I know that the capital and the country will rise to the occasion, even if at times it is a bit of a squash on the Piccadilly underground!

A completely new area of interest emerged when my friend Rajan Jetley, the former chairman of Air India, introduced me to Subash Chandra, chairman of ZeeTV who appointed me to his main board. Subash is a tremendous entrepreneur and his company has made a big impact.

* * *

Readers may be wondering what I had done with my original sweets business, Bombay Halwa, while Noon Products was expanding and constantly changing hands and I was being distracted by work with my Foundation. After I sold Noon Products I decided to buy back the remaining shares of Bombay Halwa from the Suterwalla brothers. I have always felt that I do best when I am on my own, the captain of the ship. If I make a mistake it will be my fault and there will be no one else to blame. Happily my track record speaks for itself.

My partners in the business and I were getting on but there was no guarantee that our children would see eye to eye. The most sensible route available was for one side to buy out the other. So we sat down together like gentlemen and simply agreed terms. There was no animosity, no disagreement. I made an offer that was accepted and Bombay Halwa was back in my hands in its entirety. Thus the Royal Sweets business continues to this day.

Chapter Thirteen

Desert Island Discs and Family Values

I have been generously honoured and rewarded for my work in the UK, but perhaps the most quintessentially British accolade that can be offered to anyone is to be invited to be the "castaway" on the BBC's *Desert Island Discs*. The Radio 4 programme was created by the late Roy Plomley in 1942 and its format has remained unchanged. Each week a guest is invited to choose the eight records they would most like to have with them if they found themselves marooned on a desert island. On 7 March 2004 my selection was "prised" out of me by Sue Lawley, and perhaps this choice of music gives as good an understanding as anything of Noon the man rather than Noon the businessman.

While I will always remain proud to call Great Britain my home, it is impossible to take the Indian boy out of my soul, so my first choice of record – "Nat Bhairav", performed by Shivkumar Sharma – was chosen to remind me of the sounds of the Kashmiri valleys. But of course I was an Indian boy with dreams, and those dreams were usually born of my visits to the cinema. I can name most of the great film stars, particularly those of yesteryear, and to this day relish the chance of going to the movies. I do not think I missed a single film starring Dean Martin so it was natural that I should choose his "Gentle on my Mind" to remind me of those magical youthful days.

Desert Island Discs is all about remembering the past when you were not alone on the island, so you can give free rein to nostalgia. This inspired me to choose my third record, "Ae Meri Zohra Jubin" played by the pianist Brian Silas, taken from the CD *Beyond Space: Nostalgic Film Tunes*. My American adventure, of course, was not a great success, perhaps because I was trying to operate in unfamiliar territory. I was a stranger in the US, but it had its happy moments, so who better to pick next than Frank Sinatra singing "Strangers in the Night"? I was living a dream, so why not indulge those memories?

I will come to my faith in a moment, but my fifth record, the "Raga: Bageswari-Gat in Teental" played by Hariprasad Chaurasia and Zakir Hussain, is an almost spiritual piece of music, and when the going gets tough on my desert island I know this music will have a soothing effect. Even though I am busy from the moment I wake up until the time I go to bed, it is important to me to find those quiet moments of calm to reflect on what I am doing and where I am going, if nothing else.

When I drove away from the smouldering ruins of my factory wondering what on earth I was going to do, I absent-mindedly pushed a CD into the player and I heard the exquisite voice of Luciano Pavarotti singing Schubert's "Ave Maria". There was such energy in his voice that I was immediately uplifted. There was no reason to despair; no one had been hurt in the fire. Tomorrow was another day and a solution would be found.

My seventh record probably injected a little humour into the programme – Dolly Parton singing "Nine to Five". I see a soul mate in Dolly Parton, who also overcame a tough childhood to become the superstar country singer known all over the world. She also happens to be a very astute businesswoman. And yes, we both certainly worked round the clock to reach our goals.

Finally, I chose the fiery Tina Turner singing "Private Dancer" as my eighth record. Tina Turner has livened up many of my parties and this record would always remind me of my family and friends, should I ever start feeling sorry for myself.

Castaways are entitled to one luxury, and family and friends will not be surprised to hear that I asked for a collection of videos showing some of the most exciting cricket matches. I would be alone so no one could possibly complain!

Usually castaways are given the Bible but in my case I was offered the Koran and a choice of one other book to while away the time as I waited for my rescuers. I love reading biographies and autobiographies, so I chose Nelson Mandela's *Long Walk to Freedom*. He has been an inspiration to countless thousands of people around the world and surely no one can read his story about his many years of imprisonment – often in solitary confinement – without being uplifted. Not only did he thank those who freed him, but he made a point of thanking the guards and those who had deprived him of his youth. One of his guards visited him in his home some time later, and Nelson Mandela welcomed him as a guest. A remarkable man, whose story will inspire generations of readers to come.

Most of all on my desert island I would miss my family and friends, so let me talk a little about them here – not just to heap praise on them, as quite naturally I would want to do, but also to illustrate an important point about how to conduct oneself in both personal and commercial life. Trust and loyalty are a given in most families and if you can find trust and loyalty in a business then you have achieved a great deal. If everyone has the same agenda, the same focus and above all the mutual desire for success then every individual will be working for the common good. But without such trust you are doomed to failure.

Coming from a large family with many siblings I grew up with a familiarity and longing for big clan gatherings. As children, we slept within arm's length of each other; as adolescents we played with the same cricket bat; as adults we spend quality time together in the ancestral house in Bhawani Mandi. It is natural then that I have watched the second generation grow up and have taken an avuncular interest in their future.

My sister Shirin's son, Nizar, was the first one to work with me in London. I encouraged him to move in 1988 and he became a director of Noon Products. He proved himself worthy of my trust and was a great support to me. In 2006 he resigned and he and my daughter, Zeenat, are working together on other ventures of their own in London.

My sister Kaniz's son, Naeem, came much later in 2002 from Dubai to work at Bombay Halwa and having him there has strengthened my organisation. Kaniz herself works in Royal Sweets in Mumbai. My brother,

Abbas's son, Zahid, is also at Bombay Halwa and takes care of one of the factories. Meanwhile, Akbar's son, Alexi, lived in Manchester for a time supervising our residential property interests there, while his other son, Mikael, is still studying. So the whole family is close, in fact I was "accused" by my sisters and brothers of taking away all the younger generation.

The daughters of the family have married and followed their own destinies but we keep in constant touch. Often when we descend on Bhawani Mandi with family and friends it can be quite a gathering but my brother Abbas's wife, Rehana, somehow manages to organise us all.

As I was not a very well-educated man, I was determined to surround myself with friends who could, as it were, fill in the gaps in my education. If I have any regrets it is that I missed out on formal further education. But it is only a small regret because, as I have mentioned, my mother always told me that you can judge a man by the company he keeps and, on that score, I have indeed been very fortunate.

It is invidious to pick out names. Some people that I regard as friends I have only recently met but we have managed to hit it off. Others, like Ismail Rasani, a British-trained barrister who returned to practise in India, was part of my life from the start in Mumbai; indeed, since our two fathers were friends, you might say our friendship began even before I was born. There was also my longstanding friend Vasant Vagaskar, whom I met by chance one day at the gym way back in the 1960s; we were both interested in body-building and weight-lifting.

Hunting was still permitted in India in those days and I have to say it was a great passion. I remember my elder brother, Mohammed Husain, would always be shooting, so naturally I also took up the sport with my friends, such as Anwar Khan – trekking off by bullock cart, by horse and even on camels, going off and roughing it in the jungle. My friends and I would seize every opportunity we could to get away for a few days. Of course we were completely out of touch with our families, and my mother used to get very worried but I suppose she knew we were in the safe hands of our long-serving Abdul – the man who had taught me to swim in a well.

Later I would travel in a little more comfort with another friend who had a factory next to mine in Mumbai, A.R. Kazi, who had a factory next to mine in Mumbai. He had a jeep, and we would drive miles, for a week or ten days camping in the wild. In the UK today I still go pheasant- and partridge-shooting and stalk stags during my annual holidays in Scotland.

I have many friends whom I have supported in business. After nearly half a century, I remain on the boards of their companies and often those close ties extend down through the generations. There is an invisible but unbreakable bond with such people who are there when your business hits hard times or when you have personal difficulties and tragedies. I believe this bond transcends friendship to become almost a surrogate family, providing a network of support that runs so deep that it crosses continents and spans the years. There are friends like Kausar Kazmi, at Habib Bank Zurich, who helped arrange financing on certain projects or Shabir Randeree, whom I have worked with on various property interests. They are an inspiration to me.

Tony Good, who was a co-director with me at Taj Group back in my ill-fated America days, is a wise businessman as well as a friend. We are board members together on three or four other companies and I tell him that I only have to sit with him for half an hour and I come away with something new. There are people like Mohammed Risaluddin and his wife, Sabah, whom I have known for 20 years or more. He is a good adviser and been an important guide for my speeches on Islam. And there's Uddav Thakre, the president of Shiv Sena the Hindu Nationalist political party, and son of Balasahib Thakre, the cartoonist who galvanised the people of Maharashtra to become more entrepreneurial.

Wherever we find ourselves in the world there is someone to reach out to. When I arrived in the UK the Suterwallas were there for me, father, mother and sons. Yes, I know it is typical of the way Indian society functions, the way people get involved in each other's lives. It may be too much for the more reserved western culture, but I believe all peoples can learn from these traditions. I know in British society personal lives are fiercely protected. Business is business and private is private, and never the twain shall meet; never mix business with pleasure. I can see the argument but, speaking personally, friendships have played an important part in my life and what success I have enjoyed has been in great part thanks to those friendships.

Difficulties do occur – it would be foolish to pretend otherwise – but I have another rule: I will always try to protect and preserve the friendship rather than persevere with a business relationship that has soured.

With my own immediate family there was potential for conflict and jealousy. My brother Abbas is four years older than me, my brother Akbar four years younger. Instead of being envious, they both have accepted me as the leader, and when I took over Royal Sweets in Mumbai and began building it up, they supported me. They instinctively recognised that I was the one in the family with the entrepreneurial streak, and they never got in my way. I was lucky, because I have seen sibling animosity and rivalry in some businesses and it can be highly destructive. You can settle big disputes with business rivals but it is hard when siblings fall out, I imagine because there is no way to escape from your business colleagues as they are also your brothers and sisters. So while I have looked after my siblings by ensuring that the business has grown, they too have looked after me by giving unswerving support in a wholehearted manner. As children, of course, we fought, but as adults we have never disagreed about the direction in which the various companies were going.

Mutual respect encourages you to do more for your family. You have been given the reins, so it is up to you to follow the right path; there is an obligation to reciprocate your family's trust with success. So when I got the serious money from the sale of my business I wanted to make sure that my familu were comfortable. I didn't want to feel that I was living in luxury while my brothers and sisters were struggling.

Royal Sweets in Mumbai, for example, is structured so that I don't draw anything from the business. Although I have been the major investor in the partnership, I ignored advice from my advisers that I was perfectly entitled to dilute other family shareholders' equity. Technically the advice was right, but emotionally it was wrong. If you want to be a leader you have to lead by example. If I am constantly seen to be taking what is due to me instead of sharing it among the family, I will have learned nothing from my mother's admonition that anything I have achieved I have achieved with the support of those around me. Royal Sweets in Mumbai is now in the capable hands of my younger brother-in-law, Fakhri, and my grand nephew, Aamir. Although

I am not the eldest, I am at the head of the family business – and that hierarchy, if you like, is accepted in commercial matters and not questioned. The family accept my authority because I give and never ask for anything.

If you want to be a leader, you must learn to give – but of course that also means giving orders. There has to be one captain of the ship. But you must also be prepared to delegate. God has given me the skill to run businesses by remote control. For the last thirty or forty years Paper Print and Product, my very first proper business, which I started in 1969, has been run in India by the managing director, Arif Bandukwala, the son of a close friend, Feroz Bandukwala, who has now passed away. I recruited him straight from university, and I trust him implicitly. He also controls Noon Blister Packs. Bombay Halwa Ltd in the UK is the core family business. Also forty years ago, I brought Shabbir Kanchwala over from Mumbai to run the business with me. He is the very essence of honesty and loyalty. Shabbir worked with me in Mumbai and has been with me ever since.

I have been blessed with two daughters, who having completed their education and training are involved in the business: Zeenat, with the Taj Group of hotels, and Zarmin, who after a stint with Cox and Kings is now a director of Bombay Halwa Ltd. They never gave me the usual teenage grief and seem to be aware of their obligations. I will not always be around, and they understand that they have a responsibility to ensure that the lives of our extended family do not suffer if something happens to me. Some of my Indian friends have felt sorry for me because I do not have sons. This reflects the old Indian hang-up of wanting to pass on the business on to a male heir, but I always say that I have two reliable sons-in-law, Arun Harnal and Manraj Sekhon, who are like sons to me. They are stable in their thinking and a great support to me, although they are not actually in my business. The binding factor is that the next generation are close to one another – their friends are their cousins, and I am lucky that they all get along. Perhaps it was by accident that it all worked out that way, but perhaps it is in the genes travelling down through the generations from my parents.

My wife, Mohini, merits a book to herself with all her achievements. She comes from an aristocratic family: her maternal grandmother was a *kanwarani* (princess) from the royal state of Kapurthalla, and her mother had a very privileged upbringing. One of her grandfathers was at Sandhurst Military Academy in Surrey around 1918, while her other grandfather attended medical college in England at about the same time.

Mohini has worked as a journalist, playwright and film maker. We first met when she undertook a commercial art assignment for Noon Products. The company then sponsored her to direct and write *Curry Tiffin*, a documentary on the history of India through its cuisine. Mohini has her own work and is not involved in the day-to-day activities of my business life, although she has been my guide in recent years. What is important is that she has a very caring attitude, particularly towards her parents who are not in good health and whom she visits in Delhi three or four times a year, to help to organise their lives. Mohini's father suffered a stroke twenty-one years ago and I believe they are coping so well because of her. If one of them is ill she will immediately stop whatever she is working on and go to Delhi to sort things out. I have mentioned the work of the Noon Foundation, but Mohini has her own charitable projects. She has transformed the lives of two of the children of the domestic staff at the family home in Delhi. The Kent family raised them from the age of three and four, a brother and sister, put them through private schools and sent them to college. Both have now graduated and are IT technologists, part of the new, young workforce at international company call centres in Delhi.

I believe you can tell a great deal about a person's character by the way they treat their own family. If someone has not got time for his parents, wife or children – surely those nearest and dearest to him – perhaps he will show the same uncaring attitude towards his work or his colleagues. An individual's CV can only tell you so much – they have passed their exams, they have achieved great things. It is much harder to know what they are like as people. Being able to assess someone's character can make or break a deal. The time I spent alone with Kerry Food's CEO, Flor Healy, was not to haggle over figures; it was to try to understand whether the man who wanted to buy Noon Products would actually be good for my workforce and the company ethos.

In short, my family and my friends are my ultimate strength and I leant heavily upon them when fate decided to trip me up once again.

Natania as baby (above) and young woman, with GN

With the Rt. Hon, Keith Vaz, MP

With Ajit Kerkar, former chairman of Taj Hotels and Tom Vyner, former MD of Sainsbury's.

With His Highness Shaikh Khalifa Bin Salman Al Khalifa, Prime Minister of Bahrain.

David Tennant, star of Dr Who, with the Prime Minister Gordon Brown and GN.

GN and son-in-law Arun, with Mark Ramprakash at his benefit dinner a few days after scoring his 100th century in first class cricket.

The staff at the opening of Noon Products' first plant.

With Lord Sainsbury and Bob Cooper, a director of Sainsbury's.

Hobby cook!

Chief Minister Mrs Vasundhra Raje inspects a model of Noon Hospital. l to r: Mr Dushyant Raja, MP, Dr Vivek Desai, Dr Joshi, Mr Aggarwal (the architect) and my brother Akbar.

Left: GN seated in front of (l to r) Ashok Kaul, Shabbir Kanchwalla and Akbar Shiraz.

Centre: Three brothers at the inauguration of Noon Hospital.

Below: With the Chief Minister and extended family, 4th April 208 at Noon Hospital.

With Mohammad Azharudin, former captain Indian cricket team.

Enjoying cricket – I like to keep my eye on the ball!

With Intisar Hussain and Waqar Hussain.

With my friends at a cricket match in Nottingham. l to r: Nat Puri, GN, Faroukh Engineer, Mohammad Dadabhai, Fakhruddin and Hatim Suterwalla.

GN and Freddie Flintoff.

With cricketing legend Sir Gary Sobers.

At an Asian farewell dinner for PM Tony Blair. Also in the picture: Keith Vaz, MP, and Avtar Lit.

Chapter Fourteen

CASH FOR HONOURS – THE FULL STORY

I was in Bahrain leading a delegation of businessmen promoting British industry when I heard that I was virtually being accused of trying to buy a peerage. The irony would have been amusing had it not been potentially so damaging to my reputation. The British penchant for trying to destroy anyone who seeks to do well not only for themselves but for their country is remarkable: build someone up and then knock them down. We have turned it into a peculiarly nasty British art form. Why are we so ashamed of, almost embarrassed by, success?

For me the so-called Cash for Honours affair was sixteen months of false accusation by innuendo and half-truths, and an overwhelming feeling of being let down after years of service. Although I had a completely clear conscience, no one likes to be maligned. I took comfort from my friends and from the ordinary "man in the street". On one occasion when the media were in full cry over the story, I happened to ring for a taxi. When the driver arrived, he asked if I was Sir Gulam Noon, and he said: "Can I just say that you have been treated very badly by my Party." If that was how the general public – even a Labour Party supporter – felt without any prompting from me then I was confident things would eventually work themselves out. It still took more than a year before I felt I had been cleared of any wrong-doing, and in my blackest moments I seriously considered pulling out of the country altogether.

I have had friends in all the political parties – Liberal, Conservative and Labour – ever since I arrived in Britain, which does not mean, as one journalist put it, that I was a fly-by-night political animal simply supporting whichever party happened to be in power. I did not have much money at first, but when I grew richer and found myself mixing with politicians, they became my friends. Without joining any particular party, I would help. If someone came from the Conservatives and said they needed some financial backing, I would give it to them. John Selwyn Gummer, former Tory Cabinet Minister and Secretary of State, when asked by the BBC about the whole row, said:

> If you take Sir Gulam Noon, who is a remarkable man who has transformed the area in Southall that he provides employment for, he has been a great leader for moderate Muslim thought. I'm sorry he's a supporter of the Labour Party, but he is a distinguished man who has been besmirched instead of honoured and I believe has been very seriously damaged entirely wrongly.

As regards the Labour Party, I liked them as soon as Tony Blair came to power. New Labour's policy was very simple: to make sure the unions worked in partnership with companies. As I explained, I experienced the role of unions in my own business in the late nineties. The second element of Tony Blair's attraction was that he was prepared to listen to commerce, the entrepreneurs. In other words, his was almost a Conservative Party, but with the refinement that it was not wholly anti-union, which Margaret Thatcher seemed to have become – as a result effectively suffocating one section of society. Now I accept that the unions before Thatcher had become all-powerful and there needed to be a correction, but the correction she made went too far. Don't get me wrong – I think she did a fantastic job. The unions had become too extreme and were creating chaos in the country: we had the three day week, which I experienced in my factories.

So gradually New Labour brought the unions back into the fold, and people who joined a company had the right to ask for union recognition, provided that the majority of workers felt the same way. (The Fairness at Work Act was passed in 1999.) As a result, today the unions are working with management, not against them; there is a balance. Then Labour brought in the minimum wage, which was also very important. I think that it was a brave and correct decision because people were being exploited in some industries.

It was this style of inclusive government that attracted me to New Labour, and my first formal contact with the Party organisation was around 2000 when a long-standing family friend, Keith Vaz MP, who was already rising through the Party ranks himself, introduced me to Margaret McDonagh, later Baroness McDonagh, General Secretary of the Labour Party. As I recall, I met Margaret over dinner one evening and was impressed by what I heard, and that is when I started making donations – my first cheque was for £50,000. I continued to make donations when I was approached, but I never went to any politician for a favour – either business or personal. I was making money, and the law allows you to support whichever party you like, so I was just doing what was legally permissible. As I saw it, a friend was asking me for help and I was in a position to give it. The motivation was the same as for my Noon Foundation.

It was all very casual. Keith and Margaret simply explained that the party needed funds, and I offered to help because I could. And yes, it made me feel good. Which human being, whether a businessman or a bureaucrat or a company secretary, would not like to hobnob with the politicians who are in power? Power is an aphrodisiac and power ultimately lies in Westminster, so why would I not want to move in those circles? If the Attorney General of the day happens to be walking past and says, "Hello, Gulam. How are you?", my ego is boosted. I do not need anything from him and he certainly does not need anything from me.

It is like when you go to a restaurant and the maître d' asks whether you have a reservation. Perfectly correct, but if he greets you with, "Hello, Sir Gulam. How are you today?" – immediately you feel ten times taller. It's perfectly natural, and your guests are suitably impressed. It all comes down to recognition. If anyone says he does not like to be recognised, he is a liar. Everyone likes recognition – and so do I. We are all egotistical and I am no exception. But as long as you do not misuse a friendship, no harm is done. Once you start abusing your influence you are in trouble – I also know a lot of politicians in India but I do not go with a request for them to do this or that.

Life is full of recognition. I was travelling in an aircraft recently and one of my fellow passengers was Mohanlalji Mittal, father of the steel billionaire Lakshmi Mittal. I have always admired Mohanlalji Mittal and he wrote a charming letter to me on our return. I wrote back saying that as long as there are people like him, who despite all their wealth still care about the downtrodden, there is hope. On another occasion, when a taxi driver had seen a documentary in which I featured he said it was fantastic and refused to charge me! But I insisted because he was doing his job.

Anyone, whether a multi-millionaire or a taxi driver, needs acknowledgement. It says that a person took the trouble to remember you. It is a common courtesy, and everyone likes these extra touches. People work all their lives to pay their mortgages and taxes and educate their children – and in the end all they want is recognition.

My long working life in business, my charitable and social work, and my engagement with politics have brought me recognition. When I was at a function at Buckingham Palace shortly after I had been knighted, there were a lot of people present. Prince Charles came straight over to me and said how pleased he was that I had been knighted.

Of course recognition comes at a price. It can be dangerous. Benazir Bhutto should have seen the writing on the wall before returning to Pakistan in 2007. Before she left I predicted that she would not come back; I told her solicitor, who is also my friend, Sarosh Zaiwalla. It was a simple analysis. She was making all that noise about going to end extremism and close the madrassas. That was as good as a signal to the extremists that she was an agent in the pay of the CIA. America is coming to rule us – remove her! And then her ego was her downfall. The day she arrived there was a bomb blast that killed about 250 people; she should have learned her lesson. At the next rally she was travelling with her head out of the car sunroof when there was another explosion, and some say a gunshot. Whatever the cause, she died. It was a tragic and needless waste of a life. Sarosh called me straight away and said my warning had been right.

★ ★ ★

My financial relationship with the Labour Party is scarcely the stuff of great conspiracies. The drama was over methodology. The first ball was bowled back in 2004 by Lord Levy, known as "Lord Cashpoint" by the media for his ability to raise millions of pounds for New Labour. Tony Blair decided to appoint Lord Levy as party fundraiser as the party had effectively run out of cash and would need to fill its coffers before the impending 2005 general election. It was feared that the Conservative Party would simply outspend Labour and win the election as a result.

Lord Levy, Tony Blair's tennis partner and personal Middle East envoy, came up with a plan to approach wealthy Labour supporters and ask for donations. It was also suggested that funds should be raised in the form of loans although it was reported that Levy was initially against the idea because eventually loans have to be repaid with interest. It was an idea said to have been borrowed from Lord Marland, the Tory Treasurer, who managed to borrow millions to replenish Conservative Party funds – contributions had apparently dried up when the party was going through some of its bleakest moments under the brief leadership of Ian Duncan-Smith. All I know is that Michael Levy, a former music publisher, was very good at his job and within months had raised some £14 million, but there again he was pushing at a series of open doors. He knew all the people to approach who were at least sympathetic to the Labour cause and he was presumably given the go-ahead to raise the money by Tony Blair.

I cannot speak for anyone else, but as far as I was concerned the Levy technique was nothing if not frank. Like many others, I have been invited to the Levy home in Mill Hill, North London. I went to three dinner parties there with other guests – all of us potential donors. Everyone knew why they were invited: it was not to sample Lord Levy's food, but so that we could get out our cheque books. It was simple: don't go if you don't want to give. I was happy to give. To me politics is like watching a cricket match – it is always more exciting if you care which side is going to win. I wanted to see Labour win; I had a real interest in the result. At every election I am awake all night – I never sleep. I sit up watching the results coming in, just as I will also get up at 4.30 in the morning to watch a cricket match on the television. It is the difference between being interested and being just a casual observer.

Apart from my focus on business, I am keenly interested in the society in which I live. I am I suppose a clubbish sort of fellow and enjoy working voluntarily for organisations where I can make a difference. I love sports and support benefits for cricketers, in particular, in the same way. (I collect signed cricket bats and have so many that they threaten to crowd me out of my office.) And, yes, I enjoy politics. Long before I came to London I was active in local politics in Mumbai. I also make time to give talks to young people, such as a recent one I gave at Eton College on entrepreneurship. Who knows – I might have been addressing a future Prime Minister. If I can touch one human being, my job is done.

The contribution that caused all the fuss as far as I was concerned came early in 2005. Lord Levy called me one Saturday morning and asked if we could meet. I said I had another engagement but I could see him for ten minutes. I went to his house, and with his typical frankness he told me that the party needed some money for the election. I said I would be happy to give £30,000 or £40,000. But he said no, he needed a big sum – a million pounds. I said I could not give that amount, and that is when he explained that it could be in the form of a loan. A loan was different, so I said I would lend £200,000 as an interest-bearing loan. He twisted my arm and I agreed to pay £250,000. And that was that. I left and went off to my other appointment. There was no talk of anything else. He did not assure me of any position in political life and I never expected him to. Journalists say that there was a nod and a wink, but there was not, and he had no authority to give any such assurance. He was not in a position even to wink.

Michael Levy, as I have always maintained, is a good man and he did nothing wrong. He was asked by the Prime Minister of the day to perform a task – which he did with considerable success, I might add. If he used the system and the law to the Party's benefit, so be it. If people do not like a system, it should be changed; but never blame the people who use the system as it stands. Some of the MPs sitting in Parliament should thank him because he raised the money that enabled them to fight the campaigns that got them elected. He earned nothing out of it. On the contrary, it must have cost him money. From my point of view it was a perfectly sensible financial transaction and, as far as I could tell, one without risk! How wrong can you be?

I was delighted when in May 2005 Labour won its third consecutive victory under Tony Blair, albeit with a reduced majority, and once again I focused on my business life. Some months later I learned that Lord Janner of Braunstone QC had proposed my name as a new working peer. Needless to say I was thrilled, but I was also taken by surprise. I had not requested nomination, and nor had I ever expected it. The initiative was entirely someone else's. If people thought I could make a contribution in the House of Lords – which with all due modesty I think I could have done – I was very happy to accept. After all, I was no longer burdened with the day-to-day running of my business and I would have had time to attend the House regularly. The mistake that so many commentators made at the time was in thinking that I was pushing for the title. If you remove that from the equation then the logic that I was trying to buy something – when I had not asked for, lobbied for or even hinted at desiring it – simply collapses. I know everything has its price, but who really believes that you can buy a peerage for £250,000? As I have said, if peerages came that cheaply people would be queuing round the corner of Downing Street, cheque books in hand. It would laughable if the accusation were not potentially so destructive.

So I was not happy when on 23 October 2005 the *Independent on Sunday* got hold of a leaked list of nominations for peerages and the Cash for Honours story was underway with its accusations of cronyism. Blair, the media said, was deeply involved in exactly what he had pledged to eliminate – namely sleaze. The mud was flying, and other people whose names were on the list were hit including of Dr Chai Patel, owner of the Priory Clinics, Sir David Garrard, the property developer, Biotech tycoon Sir Christopher Evans of Merlin Biosciences and Barry Townsley, a stockbroker.

There were two problems. One concerned the peerage nomination forms we all had to complete showing our financial relationship with political parties. To my way of thinking the question was very clear. I had to declare all my financial dealings with all political parties, and I instructed my accountant, Mr Selva, to draw up the list, which naturally included the loan for £250,000. He hand-delivered the form to Richard Roscoe, a civil servant at 10 Downing Street, for forwarding to the Lords Appointments Commission, chaired by Lord Stevenson. The next morning, Michael Levy rang to enquire whether I had submitted the form. I said yes, and then he asked me if I had mentioned the amount of £250,000 and I confirmed that I had. Without any prompting he pointed out that I was not obliged to mention that amount since it was a commercial interest-bearing loan.

I am certain that Michael rang me. My brother, Akbar, and Mr Selva were in my office and both of them heard the conversation. Subsequently, during the police inquiry, they checked both my office and mobile phone bills and there was no record of my having dialled Lord Levy's number at the time.

Now Michael's view of events differs slightly from mine. He suggests that I mistakenly declared the loan and called him to ask his advice on how to correct the error. And it is suggested in a separate note that he would have been perfectly happy for me to declare the loan. Whatever his recollection, I do know that he called me and the result was that I asked Downing Street to return my original application, which I amended as per Michael's directions. Hair-splitting you might think, but our accusers would say that it all goes to the real intent. Were we deliberately trying to deceive and cover up the transaction or was it a simple correction of an innocent error?

This gets to the heart of the second problem – the feeling that Labour were trying to get round their own rules about declaring any donation over £5,000. Having been transformed into loans, the donations did not need to be declared – apparently.

If there is a problem in the peerage process it is not my fault. I did exactly what the Labour Party told me to do in writing. Matt Carter, General Secretary to the Labour Party, wrote to me on Labour Party Head Office paper dated 20 April 2005 stating:

> The agreed interest rate is broadly equivalent to the Party's normal cost of funds and therefore can be considered as a commercial rate of interest. Accordingly, the loan will not give rise to any reportable

donation within the meaning of the Political Parties, Elections and Referendums Act 2000.

Who am I to argue? I would have assumed that they would have checked with their solicitors. In plain English, it was a complete cock-up. I do not know why the Labour Party – any party – should want to conceal who their financial supporters are, assuming that they are all above aboard, so I do not go along with the elaborate conspiracy theory. People were just following the rules. The Labour Party should have informed the Appointments Commission, who scrutinise all nominations for such honours, that there were loans involved and the Commission could have said that any loans must also be listed under the section concerned with financial relationships.

Even now I am baffled by the thinking in the Party. Why were we allowed to be humiliated by the press? The Prime Minister's office sent me a form; I sent it back. The Labour Party say in writing that loans are not reportable. Am I going to challenge the mighty Labour Party, who presumably have armies of legal and financial advisers? And yet the question was very simple: "What is your financial relationship with political parties?" So I put the loan down in the form. There cannot have been any coordination between the Labour Party and the Appointments Commission, so that is why I go for the cock-up theory.

We were all victims. We did not ask to be nominated. The Prime Minister chose the names and he is not so foolish as to just pick any name out of a hat: he must have applied his mind and taken advice.

The whole business of funding political parties has to be sorted out. In America each candidate raises millions of dollars, and we cannot go down that road. But there has to be some way for a political party to fight an election whether it is by taxing individuals £10 each or some other method. The money has to come from somewhere. We liked the Labour Party; we could afford to help, so it was perfectly logical that we should be asked.

I remember the Prime Minister, on a tour of Lebanon, asking why he should not reserve seats for people who support the party. He went that far. Throughout history the rulers of England, whether kings, queens or prime ministers, have given favours and rewards to those who support them. That has always been their prerogative and everyone understands that it happens.

Supporting a party with money is an important element – as I always say, there is no substitute for money. It happens all over the world. It goes without saying that parties will think first of their big supporters and backers when it comes to making appointments, and that includes working peers. There is no harm done as long as the people are competent and are not "buying" the reward. It is allowed by law. Frankly, I believe that both Houses of Parliament should be filled with people with real life business experience, not party animals who have known nothing else but politics. In days gone by people went into politics to do some good, and many did not even need the money. Today it seems to be about ambition, higher expenses and a good salary.

My own conscience is completely clear and I believe that I did nothing wrong. The error was quite simply between the Labour Party and the Appointments Commission. But once the hare had been set running there was no stopping the chase. First of all the Appointments Commission blocked Chai Patel's and Sir David Garrard's nominations, then in March 2006 my nomination was also blocked. I heard the news, as I say, when I was in Bahrain trying to do my bit for my country. My mobile lit up with calls from the press wanting my reaction, and they were there to "doorstep" me when I returned to Heathrow. I explained that I would not be making any statement then but that I would give my reaction in the morning.

That night I worked late in my office in St James's, trying to decide on the best course of action. With me were my wife, Mohini, my daughter, Zarmin, the ever loyal Keith Vaz and my solicitor. The atmosphere was gloomy to say the least. All around us from the walls and shelves the faces of family, friends and, yes, politicians of every persuasion, in paintings and photographs, looked down on our deliberations. With their support and guidance so much had been achieved, and yet now there was a real possibility that it would all crumble to dust.

We thrashed out all possible reactions. I said that I had worked hard for the country and paid my taxes, had not asked for any favours in return – and this was the thanks I got. Quitting the country altogether was mentioned, but only in a fit of pique. I did not blame the Labour Party for the furore but they were clearly at fault for the chaos. It was unfortunate, and driven perhaps more by the media. Things had to be kept in perspective, and as always I wanted to stay focused on my work and not let anything damage the smooth running of the company.

Eventually it was clear what had to be done. There was only one problem and it had to be dealt with swiftly. So in the morning I sent a note to the Prime Minister, with a copy to the Appointments Commission, withdrawing my name. Many of my friends including those in the press like Amit Roy were dismayed – he wrote an article headlined: "Noon should go to the House of Lords." To me the most important thing was to behave in an honourable and dignified manner, which I think I did. That is when I asked to see Tony Blair at Downing Street to get him to pull me out of the mess.

Every day during March 2006 seemed to bring a new headline. The Scottish Nationalist MP Angus MacNeil made a formal complaint to the Metropolitan Police that the awards – or potential awards – might have breached the 1925 Honours (Prevention of Abuses) Act, and this was taken seriously enough for a formal investigation under Deputy Assistant Commissioner John Yates to be launched. Parliament was told to postpone its own public grilling of some of the key players – Chai Patel was apparently only too eager to appear before MPs to tell them exactly what had happened. He, like the rest of us, was furious about the way in which events were unfolding; we seemed to be powerless to stop the daily abuse and accusations. There was also a very real worry that we might all end up in prison. At least we might have been in good company, as it was not long before the Prime Minister himself came under the forensic scrutiny of John Yates and his team.

Everyone involved – including 10 Downing Street – was sent letters formally requesting all relevant documentation. There seemed to be wholesale chaos in Labour Party ranks. Their own Treasurer, Jack Dromey, was furious because he had apparently been kept in the dark about the loan arrangements and there was not a little embarrassment about some of the people from whom Labour had been willing to accept money. An anonymous source quoted by the *Sunday Times* said: "What hurts much more … is to have to put us in hock to people who do not share our ideals or values."

Before March was over there was a real possibility of the police inquiry reaching as far as Downing Street and the Prime Minister himself, and eventually, early in April, Tony Blair was forced to submit a new list of working peers with the so-called secret millionaire donors – Chai Patel, Sir David Garrard, Barry Townsley and me – removed, although I of course had already withdrawn my name. But that did not put out the flames. Scotland Yard was now on the case and nothing would stop the investigation. It was not long before the first arrest was made – Des Smith, a former government schools adviser who recruited wealthy backers for city academies was quoted by an undercover reporter as saying that donors could be recommended for honours, including peerages. He had already resigned over the story, but John Yates wanted to learn more and in July there was the ignominious moment when Lord Levy was arrested for questioning. His London home was searched and various documents were seized. Sir Christopher Evans of Merlin Biosciences was also arrested and later released. In due course I too received a knock on the door from Yates's men.

The police twice interviewed me under caution. The first time they came to my solicitor's office. They showed extraordinary courtesy and I had great respect for them – they were simply doing their job. I told them what was already in the public domain and it was clear, I hope, that I had nothing to hide from them. The second time they came to my office in St James's, and again they could not have been more polite. This time they brought with them certain confidential papers that they were obliged to show me. They gave me a sensitive file and allowed me to sit alone to study the papers in my own room, and that impressed me. I could have taken the papers and shredded them, but they trusted me and I found that very comforting.

People are critical of the police but I always say that, just like businessmen who make mistakes, they also make mistakes from time to time. They are not supermen. Yates was given a tough assignment – constantly in the spotlight and highly politically charged – and he just got on with it. How can you blame anyone in that position? It just took a long time.

Of course, as we now all know, there were other arrests. Ruth Turner,

Number 10's Director of Government Relations, was "picked up" in a bizarre dawn raid on her home – which seemed unnecessary – and Tony Blair became the first sitting Prime Minister to be questioned by the police in a criminal investigation. There was real pressure on him to step down early; he had already indicated that he was going to resign but had not yet set a date. I know from personal conversations that he was reluctant to go because he wanted to leave at a time and in a manner of his own choosing.

There is no doubt that the Cash for Honours saga cast a cloud over the final weeks of his premiership, and the fact that sixteen months and about £1 million later the Crown Prosecution Service (CPS) announced on 20 July 2007 that no one would be charged simply added to the bad taste left in everyone's mouth. The conspiracy theorists cried "cover-up". The Labour Party as a whole must have felt their reputation had at the very least been badly damaged. The few of us who had been cast as the villains of the piece wondered what on earth the whole thing had been about – the endless sleepless nights, the accusations and the hours wasted with lawyers and other advisers. My family, friends, business associates and simply individuals who barely knew me had looked on in astonishment, anger and bemusement as the sorry saga worked itself out.

Overwhelmingly I felt let down. Tony Blair was quoted as saying that those who had been questioned had been through "a terrible, even traumatic time". In particular my friends in India were astounded because they could not understand the political game being played. They knew what I had achieved in the UK and the voluntary and charitable work I had done. If this was the way that politicians treated their supporters, what fate lay in store for their enemies?

The CPS statement said that no "agreement" to exchange money for a peerage could be proved and, crucially as far as I was concerned, that each of the businessmen on Tony Blair's list of potential peers was "a credible candidate for a peerage". The House of Commons Public Administration Select Committee's own report on Propriety and Peerages also absolved us, and I was delighted that my written submission to the committee was printed in full in the official report, which will stand as a formal historical record:

LETTER TO THE CHAIRMAN FROM SIR GULAM NOON, DATED 11 AUGUST 2006

I hope that the Committee does not mind if I send this personal letter. I write to the Committee because it is investigating the honours system in this country, and because some time ago I was asked to give oral evidence before it and my profile in relation to a potential peerage is very much in the public domain.

I had hoped that, by now, I would have appeared before the Committee. For reasons which I, of course, understand, that appearance has not taken place. In the circumstances, I think that it is right to provide this letter. I do not regard what I set out below as confidential.

I first of all would like to set out my background, my present life and business. My reputation is of great importance to me. It has been built up over 50 years of which 37 have been spent in this country. Through what I consider no fault of mine, I now find myself in the invidious position of having to defend it.

I have always acted honourably in my working life. I am in the business of ready-made meals and I think I can claim the credit of creating Britain's favourite dish, chicken tikka massala. My factories are in the Ealing and Southall area and I employ over 1000 people in what is a semi-deprived area.

I serve on various public bodies: The Covent Garden Market Authority from 1995–2001, London TEC and presently the Transport for London Committee (appointed on 1 March 2004). I am on the board of certain charities – CARE International UK from 2002–2006 and The advisory Council of The Prince's Trust since 1996. I have also been a member of The Advisory Board on Nationalisation and Integration (ABNI) since 2004.

I believe that every individual has a responsibility to give back to society, in terms of both time and money. That is our social contract. My own charitable trust, the Noon Foundation, was created in 1999 with a personal contribution of £4 million. We do not actively raise any funds from the public. The Foundation has been engaged in several projects. As one example, it supported a mentoring scheme for young people at Tower Hamlets College for over three years, 2000–2003, with a contribution of £200,000. I do not limit myself to my own charity. I actively support The Prince's Trust.

130

Nor do I limit myself to charitable or political giving. I gave Norwich City Football Club £100,000. Delia Smith, a director, is a personal friend. I gave the same amount to Surrey County Cricket Club towards a new stand and underwrote a further £400,000 for the India Room. I hope these facts put my political loan in some context. The Labour Party needed funds before the next election. I was asked to help and was able to do so. To my mind, there is no connection between that loan and the eventual approach in relation to a peerage.

I would have been immensely honoured to be granted the opportunity to work in the House of Lords. I perhaps immodestly feel that I have made a good contribution to society and now at 70 years of age and at a stage in my business life where I would have devoted considerable time to the House, I would have been pleased to do the work. Certain issues would have been close to me. For example, although I am a Muslim, after the July 7th bombing, I wrote articles which criticised terrorists. There are a number of areas where I feel that I could have made a contribution to the work of the House.

Having said that, I am very anxious to make it entirely clear that I have never made a political or any other donation or loan with a view to any kind of honour. I have been honoured before. In 1994, I was awarded the MBE under the Conservative government; in 2002, I received a Knighthood and, in January this year, the President of India gave me a "Gold Medal" award for my contribution to that society. I was involved in charitable projects such as the building of hospitals and schools in my native state of Rajasthan, India. I am quite certain that none of these honours was in any way connected with any loan given by me at any time. I hope that in the past, and now in relation to the recommendation for a peerage, it has been my work over the years which is the real reason why I have been awarded or put forward.

My loan to the Labour Party came about because of the Party's need for general election funds. Lord Levy asked me if I could help. I was in a position to do so and offered a gift which would have been in the region of £50,000. Lord Levy indicated that he would prefer more and a loan of £250,000 with interest was agreed. The loan was repayable and the agreement contains terms as to interest which I regard from my point of view as commercial and the Party described it as such. The matter was agreed before the election and only arose when interest fell due. After correspondence and discussions, I added the interest to the capital sum.

I emphasise, there was no connection between this loan and the eventual recommendation of my name for a peerage.

When I was approached in relation to the possible peerage, I completed what I understood to be the usual form and disclosed on an attached document my schedule of donations including the £250,000 loan. I was, thereafter, reminded by Lord Levy that this should not have been declared because it was a loan, not a donation. At his suggestion, I telephoned Richard Roscoe, the appropriate civil servant at 10 Downing Street, and, following discussion, I wrote enclosing the revised schedule. I thought I was correcting an error and am embarrassed and upset by the nature of some of the publicity which has resulted.

I have done absolutely nothing wrong with regard to any donation or this loan.

It takes years to build a reputation but only a few hours to destroy it. It is very hard to explain to my international business associates, particularly in India, what has happened in Britain in the past few months. I felt that, when the publicity became so great, it would be right for me to withdraw my consent to nomination for a peerage. I hope that the Committee will understand how I felt.

I hope that the above information contained in this letter assists the Committee. I regard this as an open letter and I make it in the spirit of cooperation and an attempt to help. I have intended to do that from the start. I am only sorry that I have not yet been able to assist the Committee by an attendance before them.

I feel that so much anguish could have been avoided if a little commonsense had prevailed earlier on. Should the police investigation have lasted so long? I am not an expert on police procedures, although "informed sources", as they say, close to Deputy Assistant Commissioner John Yates and his team made it clear that the politicians only had themselves to blame for prolonging the inquiry. As for Lord Levy, he said it was a time for relief rather than recrimination and he got on with writing his own autobiography.

Having vowed never to pay another penny to a political party after what I and my family had been through, I calmed down and have decided that I will in effect write off my £250,000 loan and convert it into a donation to the Labour Party, now under the leadership of Gordon Brown. Like all political parties, Labour needed money – in fact they faced debts of £20 million, including £14 million of outstanding loans according to the Electoral Commission's figures. Funnily enough, the day I announced that I was prepared to give money to Labour again, I got a call from David Sainsbury who jokingly said I had beaten him to the punch as he had been on the point of donating £2 million. Lord Sainsbury, a former Science Minister in the Labour government, had also been questioned as a witness in the Cash for Honours saga, but he said he remained steadfast in his support for the Party.

What lessons should I draw from those torrid sixteen months in the hostile glare of media and police spotlights? What lessons should anyone draw when they find themselves falsely accused? It is easy to say now, when the threat has gone away, but I like to think that ultimately I drew strength from my clear conscience. I knew I had done nothing wrong and I was always confident that, should it have come to a court case, I would have been vindicated, although that did not stop me fuming every morning when I read the newspapers. I had supreme confidence in my lawyer and friend David Robinson and his team. He and I will now have an endless topic of conversation when we go on our shooting holidays in Scotland.

I have accepted that the Cash for Honours saga will continue to haunt me, probably until my dying day; maybe it will even be brought up again when my obituary is written. Far away from the Westminster scene, at home in India, there is still, and will no doubt always remain, utter confusion about the case. It is always mentioned by journalists, not out of malice but in search of clarity and understanding. A long, detailed account will never be read in Bhawani Mandi, Delhi or Mumbai. When people make accusations they should think carefully first. It is no use just saying sorry: they should consider the long-term consequences. To misquote the wartime admonition: "Careless talk costs reputations."

I was delighted when many months later, by coincidence, John Yates and I found ourselves at the same function. To avoid causing him any embarrassment I did not approach him, but he came straight up to me and warmly shook my hand. He made a point of saying how much he admired the way I had conducted myself throughout the inquiry. I was happy to tell him how professional and courteous his officers were on both occasions when they visited me.

It would be an understatement to say that I was distracted from my work during this time, although I always tried to keep my eye on the ball that mattered, which was my business life. You have to remember to concentrate on the essentials: your family, your friends and your work. Never compromise, never retaliate when you are provoked and, to use a cricketing metaphor, play with a straight bat. Speak plainly, frankly and honestly and, no matter what people say about you, in the end the truth will prevail. Not only will you learn a great deal about yourself, your strength of character and your determination, but you will quickly learn who your real friends are. Fires have threatened my businesses and literally destroyed my factories, yet I have fought back; so too is the real mettle of our character tested in other fires throughout life – sadness, setback, disappointment, even false accusation. I have emerged from this latest test of my character with, I suppose, a renewed serenity. I am still smiling. To borrow that choice phrase from a previous political debacle: "Don't let the buggers get you down!"[1]

Less than a month after Tony Blair stood down on 27 June 2007, handing over the premiership to Gordon Brown and taking up a new role in the Middle East, he kindly wrote to me. His words are self-explanatory as can be seen from his letter (*see facing page*).

---

[1] This was the phrase the Conservative MP, Michael Mates had inscribed on a watch he gave Asil Nadir, who fled to Cyprus in 1993 rather than face charges related to the collapse of his Polly Peck empire. Mates resigned over his links with Nadir.

The Office of Tony Blair

From the Rt Hon Tony Blair

24th July,

dea Gulam,

Thank you so much for your extraordinarily kind letter. You have been such a good freind to me, even though I have put you through such difficulty. I have now new challenges. The Middle East and, of course the Inter-Faith Foundation. I would love you to be involved in both and hope we can meet again soon.

In the mean time,

PO Box
London
W2 7JU

(continued overleaf)

thank you again, thank you also
for the great work you do and
please send my love to Mohini;

yours ever,

Tony

Chapter Fifteen

A VIEW ON LIFE IN BRITAIN

I feel it was typical of Tony Blair's tenacity, infectious optimism and plain courage that he was prepared to take on the poisoned chalice of the Middle East.[1] I wonder who else would have been prepared to try to sort out the monumental problems that transcend the region's borders and affect every part of the world – and not least the UK.

As an unintentionally prominent figure in the Muslim community, I seem to have become an unofficial spokesman. I see myself as speaking up for "the silent majority" of law-abiding Muslims in Britain – very few seem keen to raise their heads above the parapet. I have criticised anyone preaching sedition and treason. In open letters and articles I have said that such people should be stripped of their British citizenship and sent back to the country from which they came. There should be training programmes for British imams that "should include knowledge of English and a rigorous enforcement of entry regulations to Britain as well as the implementation of rigorous anti-terrorist laws".

I met Prime Minister Blair a couple of times in the run-up to the war in Iraq, in which I was all for prompt and decisive military action. I remember

---

[1] Within hours of his resigning as Prime Minister, it was announced that Tony Blair had been appointed special representative for the peace-broking quartet of the United States, Russia, the United Nations and the European Union.

attending a function at the Hilton Hotel. When Tony Blair walked in he turned to my daughter, Zarmin, who was accompanying me and said, "Do you know your father saved me in our last meeting?" It was when a group of Muslim leaders had met him shortly before the Iraq War; most of them were against going but I said we should move without delay. My view was and remains that Saddam Hussein had to be removed because the Iraqi people were living in fear. When he was US President in 1991, Bush senior said, after throwing the Iraqi forces out of Kuwait, that it was now up to the people of Iraq to topple him, but it would never have happened because, as in all dictatorships, the people were terrified.

In three paragraphs, that is where I stand. Let me in these next few pages explain in more detail my approach to three of the hottest topics facing the UK, and for that matter most other countries in the world – education, integration and terrorism. In my view they are inextricably linked. First of all I will look at the Iraq story because it has had an impact on all our lives. Some would indeed argue that the fact that we live in fear of terrorist attack is in large part a direct result of the second Iraq war.

Although I was for the invasion of Iraq, principally to overthrow Saddam Hussein on the basis of the information we were given, there is no denying the disastrous outcome of that war. Britain is now alongside America and squarely in the sights of the coalition of Al Qaeda and the Taliban. While terrorism was certainly the major threat of the day, all the evidence now shows that Iraq had nothing to do with 9/11. Some well-placed critics argue that George W. Bush was simply bent on attacking Iraq regardless.[2] The only outcome seems to have been the uniting of different terrorist groups against us. Germany and France were clever and did not participate in the second Gulf War; nor was their relationship with America, or for that matter with Britain, destroyed as a result.

I remain firm that it was right to overthrow Saddam Hussein because for years he ruled his people through the barrel of a gun and inflicted great

---

[2] In his book *Against All Enemies*, Richard A. Clarke, who served three US Presidents on the National Security Council Staff, is highly critical of President George W. Bush for attacking Iraq on the pretext of linking the country to 9/11.

suffering. Dictators and all tyrants are astute; they rule by fear, and that is how they succeed. The first Gulf War made sense but the coalition should have killed Saddam. The reason we did not was because the United Nations mandate only allowed us to throw him out of Kuwait. But what about the penalty? He had marched into Kuwait, raped the country and then just walked away. A burglar breaks into your house and steals something: is it right that he should just give back what he has taken, and all is then forgiven? What about punishment? That is why the second Gulf War happened, I am convinced. It was a case of unfinished business, driven by the old guard of George Bush senior who were advising his son.

With the luxury of hindsight, one can say that the job should have been finished the first time round and we could have debated the rights and wrongs afterwards. It would certainly have been a preferable outcome to what we and the Iraqi people are suffering today. While I supported the second Gulf War – and in private conversations with Tony Blair I urged him "to finish this man off once and for all" – we had no follow-up strategy. They disbanded the Baath Party and dismissed the police and army. But these men all had families to feed and now they had no source of income. We turned from liberators into conquerors in the eyes of Iraqis, and those policemen and soldiers were largely innocent. If the majority are not considered innocent then the whole population should have been killed because they were all guilty of not rising up against Saddam.

You could not hold down a worthwhile job in Iraq under Saddam without being a member of the Baath Party. Most of the population were ordinary men and women simply trying to survive with a gun pointing at them all the time. By throwing everyone out of work we made them turn against the coalition and join forces. They were a bunch of men with no jobs and plenty of weapons – a dangerous mix. I feel there was no proper briefing of the administrators who went with the army about what should happen after the defeat of Saddam. The Iraqi military and police should have been told: "The country is free of Saddam – now we must protect the people. Police, do your job and help us restore basic law and order for the citizens."

America is the senior partner and the responsibility lies there. If the war and its aftermath had been conducted in the way that I suggest then I do not believe 9/11 would have happened. As I write this, there are some signs that gradually the mood is becoming more positive; while the Iraqis are still anti the coalition forces, most want them to stay until a basic infrastructure and a strong army and police force are in place. Even more encouraging is a mood swing against the bully-boy tactics of the Taliban. We can only hope.

Looking at the picture in the UK, I will focus first on education – surely the foundation of everything. I want to start by singing the praises of teachers everywhere. Those with a genuine passion to inspire all students of whatever age simply to seek more knowledge should be treasured. In ancient times teachers were revered in all societies: the pursuit of knowledge should be encouraged and admired. In Islam the Prophet Mohammed (pbuh) was crystal clear on the matter. He urged his followers to "go in search of knowledge even unto China", and he said, "Who so honoureth the learned, honoureth me", and also, "Seek knowledge from the cradle to the grave." The message is plain enough.

I am fortunate in being able to fund schools and colleges both in the UK and in India. I have helped with renovation and extension work at four schools in the Sunel and Bhawani Mandi regions and contributed to a multi-purpose recreational complex in Bhawani Mandi. I have already mentioned the Tower Hamlets and Birkbeck College initiatives in London. There is a common denominator between all these that attracts me and it is the overwhelming desire among students to learn and improve themselves. I remember writing a letter to the press in 2004 saying that education was the "crying need of the hour". In fact I would say that education is forever the need of the hour. Even today in my seventies I try to learn from everyone I meet. Only by listening and learning can we avoid the mistakes of the past and improve ourselves.

British education is free to the masses and should be seized with both hands by everyone privileged to be offered it, but what do we see happening? It is being abused. I could not stay silent when a young teenage Muslim girl had the temerity to take her school to court because the authorities refused to allow her to wear a full-length hijab to school. I said at the time, and I repeat it now, that such an action was a flagrant abuse of her privileges as a British subject. Had she, or the people who encouraged her in this foolish challenge, not stopped for one minute to think about and appreciate the many gifts that British society had bestowed on her free of charge? Not only did she have the right to a full education but she had a free health service at her disposal and the opportunity to fulfil all her dreams as an individual, follow any career and travel where she pleased. No doubt her parents had moved from Bangladesh precisely to enjoy these privileges, and what is her response to such beneficence? To scorn the generosity and claim somehow that her rights were diminished. This misguided girl's own school had gone out of its way to consult the local Council of Mosques about appropriate dress because so many children in its catchment area were Muslims and as a result had permitted its pupils to wear salwar-kameez to class. I wrote to the principal of the school saying that I would be prepared even to pay for her tuition fees if she wanted extra help to catch up.

But these are the sad stories of the Muslim community. The girl – or rather those who hid behind her – was simply demonstrating arrogance and contempt for the school's rules and regulations and towards the country whose privileges she and they were enjoying. But these young people are being used by the imams for their own benefit. I will not change my opinion on that. The imams are indoctrinating the younger generation and bringing pressure on them and their families.

The blame lies not with the children but with the adults who guide them. What is this so-called guidance but simply a desire on the part of the ignorant or the radicals and fundamentalists to exert control and domination? Sadly, some of these people are priests or imams. Now as a Muslim I am not for one moment decrying the hundreds of years of achievements and traditions to be found in Islam. It is important for all children to be exposed to their own traditions, religious duties and teaching – but that should be an inclusive experience and a worldly education that prepares them for the multicultural society in which we all live. Only by taking that approach can they make their way in life and achieve great things in their professions in what is a highly competitive world.

Parents should pay attention to what is being taught in their children's schools and not just absolve themselves of all responsibility. Just because a child is at school does not mean that everything they are being taught is correct. Remember the nonsense I was being told as a young boy in my madrassa about not taking sweets from Hindus, Christians or Jews! It is possible for someone to go right through their education, even to university, being thoroughly indoctrinated into extremist ways. Just because someone is educated does not mean that they are enlightened; education is not the same thing as wisdom. When you go to the mosque and stand on a pedestal you are powerful and you can influence youngsters. I tell Muslims in my speeches that it is the parents' duty to ensure that their children are taught the traditional ways, prayers, and so on, but it should be under their supervision. You should not just send children off to a mosque because there is a madrassa there – you do not know what they are learning. We have seen in the UK that parents did not know when their son was being trained as a suicide bomber.

I remember giving a speech along these lines in Nottingham – men on one side, women on the other. There was an imam there, and in his talk he was actually screaming. I could not help saying in reply that, by the way he was shouting, I thought there would be a fatwa declared on somebody and probably by the end of my speech it would be against me. I said to the women that it was their duty to ensure that their children learnt the Koran and the traditions of Islam, but if they thought they were discharging their obligations just by making the children attend the madrassas they were wrong. You do not know what is happening there. Your children's education – academic and spiritual – must be under your control. At the end of my speech there was silence. No applause. Not even any facial reaction. I was a bit concerned. My loyal driver, Joginder, who was sitting at the back, said to me later that he was worried for my safety. But afterwards, while I was having dinner, a few of the women approached me and asked if I would come and talk to them. I did, and they told me that I was absolutely right but their husbands would not listen.

Why do these so-called "radical imams" promote such backward thinking as to keep women isolated from the world and in particular the world of education? In my view there can be only one reason and that is because keeping them ignorant preserves the "teacher's" lofty position.

Why are these "religious fanatics" always so ready to spill blood in God's name? I am a staunch believer that these extremists have no true religion. Their religion is terrorism, and I urge people not to bow down before terrible acts like 9/11. We have got to show these cowards that we will not be defeated by them. As a Muslim I am appalled by those who claim to be religious leaders but urge their followers to commit acts of violence. Mahatma Gandhi said: "I know of no greater sin than to oppress the innocent in the name of God."

Britain made me, with all its opportunities and benefits, and I hope every Muslim – indeed, every citizen – seizes those priceless gifts and makes the most of them. Ignore the false teachings of those few wrong-headed imams, many of whom cannot even speak English, who lead their followers astray by saying that if they become martyrs they will go to heaven where countless virgins await them. Come on, wake up! I say to the priests who preach all this: "If you are so convinced, why don't you blow yourself up and go to paradise?" My advice to all Muslims is please take care of your children and keep them away from these mad mullahs. The real culprits are not the youngsters or the ill-educated, who are easily persuaded, but the evil-minded controllers who remain at large, spreading their poison.

The difference with Islam compared to some other religions is that the imams are much more than just spiritual leaders. They also take on a social leadership that gives them enormous influence upon the minds of their congregation and the way in which they conduct themselves outside the mosques. Let the clerics focus on praying to God that he should frustrate the terrorists and protect Muslim and non-Muslim alike. Do they not read their own religious books? A teaching of the Prophet was: "The ink of the scholar is holier than the blood of the martyr." There is another important tenet of Islam that states that if you kill one human being, you kill humanity.

I must not generalise, because there are British imams who are doing an excellent job in trying to break down barriers rather than erect them, but the violent rhetoric of one Abu Hamza, the former imam of Finsbury Park Mosque in north London who personifies extremist religion for the British people, completely outweighs the patient, unseen good that is being done by others. Islam and terrorism have become joined at the hip. 'All Muslims are terrorists' is the general perception.

In fact, much of the blame lies with the British government because, in order to be politically correct, they are mollycoddling these uneducated priests. The government has a duty to protect all its citizens. Governments of all persuasions have to get tough. Naïve politicians seem to think that if they just show traditional British tolerance and a good liberal approach, extremists will eventually become like-minded. But the word "liberal" is not in these people's vocabulary. They regard tolerance as weakness and – be in no doubt – they will take advantage of such folly. There are some tentative signs that the British government is getting tougher and at least insisting that clerics should be able to speak English. It is a reflection either of their disdain for British culture or their ignorance that they have failed to grasp the language of their own volition. Whichever of these assessments is true, it must surely disqualify them from the noble profession of teacher.

I despair of the human rights activists who are always in the media spotlight protecting the very people who do not know the meaning of human rights. Abu Hamza was quick to insist on his right to free British legal aid when he had to appear in court, but not so quick to think of the rights of innocent British citizens who might have suffered as a result of his inflammatory speeches. What human rights were being displayed when terrorists blew up the bus or the trains in London on 7/7? What human rights were being shown when two planes, packed with passengers, were flown into New York's Twin Towers on 9/11, killing thousands?

Muslims should also be on their guard. They cannot just sit back and say that it is the non-Muslims who are at risk. The natural forbearance of the British will put up with so much, but one day they may say they have had enough. It will be no use claiming "I am an innocent Muslim". There will be no distinction and the question will legitimately be asked: "What did you do to stop these radicals and extremists from corrupting young minds? We didn't hear you speaking out to condemn their vitriolic sermons in the mosques."

I cannot state it any more plainly: there is no room for terrorism in religion, any religion. Love your neighbour, and show compassion towards your fellow human beings regardless of race, colour or creed: these are the teachings at the heart of every serious religion. Terrorism is all about hatred, revenge and striking back. The two are incompatible but – and it is an important but – there is nothing incompatible about Muslims, Jews, Christians or whoever living in harmony together. I grew up in Mumbai, in as mixed a bag of religions as you like, and we always got on together until, of course, the politicians became involved. Differences, where they occur, are more complex than just pure "religion"; they have also to do with economics, politics and society in general.

What you have among the peoples in Britain is diversity, not difference, and that is what makes Britain great. Diversity is Britain's greatest asset. Everyone who lives here is given the opportunity to succeed and that is why Britain – just a tiny island – is a magnet for the world. When I first came to Britain, Asians were cleaners and did other menial tasks. Today they hold ministerial positions, run banks and are among the most successful entrepreneurs in the country. When he was British Prime Minister, Tony Blair, speaking to the Confederation of Indian Industry in Bangalore, said that India's "traditions of freedom and democracy make India an obvious partner of us".

We Asians, and people of many other nationalities besides, have been accepted, even welcomed. There is therefore an obligation upon us at the very least to be polite! In December 2004 I was happy to join the Advisory Board of Naturalisation and Integration, whose job it was to offer independent advice to the government on its programme to help legal migrants integrate properly into British society. I felt it was my duty to offer such help. Sometimes that guidance has been blunt, but it is always offered in a constructive spirit. The key point, however, is that the British are reaching out to all newcomers to help them become one with the rest of society, but there is a requirement for visitors to return the gesture and seek to learn from their hosts.

In an article in the *Financial Times* in 2005 I had a blunt message for all Muslims that was equally applicable to any immigrant to Great Britain: become British and accept Britain's liberal democracy, traditions and customs, or go back to wherever you came from because you are not wanted here. What is the point of making any country your home if you do not like its ways? If they are really so offensive, leave. We are the newcomers to a land steeped in tradition. It is sheer impertinence to try to bring about changes. Can you imagine the reaction in, say, Saudi Arabia if westerners were to flout the religious laws there?

Sadly, I believe such attitudes are actually increasing in this country. I had a meeting on 23 January 2008 with the Foreign Secretary, David Miliband, and I told him the same thing. That very day in the papers there was an article about a visit to the UK by Iraq's Deputy Prime Minister, Dr Barham Salih, who had said that he was appalled at the level of fundamentalism being preached in mosques in Blackburn. He was quoted as saying: "I am not surprised that you British are facing so many problems with extremists after what I saw in those mosques in Blackburn. What I saw would not be allowed in Iraq – it would be illegal."

I have never seen people even in Mumbai wearing the burkha, with only the eyes showing. I had to come to London to witness it. I have no problem with the short hijab, but if your face is fully covered how can you expect to work as a teacher or a receptionist, or in any other position where you have to interact with others? Why should people employ you? This is a very open society. You can cover your arms and legs – that is fine – but covering your whole face in that way is not acceptable.

This situation is getting worse, and until such time as the government takes the bull by the horns it will not come to an end. The serious problem is with certain imams. Most are very good, but the few are creating fear because that is the only way they can have power. If you do this, you will go to heaven; if you do that, you will go to hell. That is why vulnerable and idealistic youngsters are becoming potential extremists and suicide bombers.

The government should put a check on these imams, and expel them if necessary. Some of them are even wanted in their own home countries. When you send them to jail you give them a room, with clean laundry and food and other facilities. Indeed, you will give them Halal food and time to pray. They will even start a congregation and convert more people to their views inside the prison.

The Home Office has the ability to grant British nationality, and in my view it has the right to throw these people out if they are not behaving. You have got to think about the whole population, not just the fifty out of 2,000 imams. If you can push them out, you will send a very powerful signal. They are not worried about going to jail, but they are very worried about going back to their homelands.

Government ministers have to realise what is happening and take a stand against these people who think that we are weak. Not only are we trying to be politically correct but we have the mistaken idea that any sort of clamp-down will spark retaliation, or even some sort of uprising among the rest of the Muslim community. This only shows how little the authorities understand the so-called minorities. The full force of the law should be applied to the extremists. When Abu Hamza was preaching in the middle of the street, having been removed from his mosque in 2003 after making speeches supporting al-Qaeda and speaking out against the invasion of Iraq, I asked David Blunkett, who was Home Secretary at the time, "Why don't you arrest him?" He said if we arrested him all the Muslims would be out on the street protesting. I told him that no more than ten people would protest – and when finally they did pick him up, no one uttered a sound.

These extremists are all bullies: desperate people who want to control others for their own ends. These imams will never tell you that if you want to read the Koran you can read it in English translation because they know that by filtering what the Koran says they can remain powerful. They will teach from their point of view. Islam is a great religion but these few people are bringing it into disrepute. When I first came to Britain there were only two mosques and now there are 1200. Islam is flourishing, so what is their problem?

Let me come back to the wearing of head-to-toe burkhas. Modesty is important in Islam but there is no rule that says women should hide their faces. In fact it is a requirement that women who perform the part of the hajj that takes them to the Ka'bah, the holiest site in Islam, actually remove their veils. How can you be a teacher or a lawyer in the courts if you do not show your face? This false modesty is even being taken up by female Muslim doctors who are said to be refusing to bare their arms when they scrub up before an operation. I simply say to my Muslim brothers and sisters that if you do this you have no hope of getting work in the European community because employers will be afraid. You may be very nice today but who says you will not go to a madrassa in the evening or at the weekend and be indoctrinated and then cause trouble later in the work place?

But I will go further. It is just as offensive in my mind to live apart in some isolated ghetto and choose to ignore people who are now your fellow countrymen. It is like going to a party and standing in a corner refusing to speak to the other guests: it would have been far better if you had never come. I have often said that I share so much of my success in life with my Hindu, Sikh, Christian, Parsi and Jewish friends. I am a passionate believer in the unity of cultures – how could I believe anything else? I come from India, a land of a billion people, where they speak more than 120 languages and are bursting with diversity.

I long for the day when my fellow Muslims truly integrate with the rest of society in Britain and, for that matter, all parts of the world. Yes, we are all different, and thank goodness for that: it is what makes the human race interesting. We are not helping ourselves, let alone the rest of the community, if we hide in our cocoons.

To achieve real integration in Britain all immigrants must positively affirm their Britishness while being able to celebrate their differences, including their religions. There is nothing wrong with a mosque in any city, but let that mosque be part of the wider community: only in that way will people of other faiths living on its doorstep cease to be so suspicious. According to academic studies reported in 2005, areas of London, Leicester, Bradford and Oldham belonged "in the major league of ethnic segregation", and Pakistani and Bangladeshi communities were among the most poorly integrated. Staggeringly, reports claimed that if immigration ended immediately it would still take forty years for all these people to be assimilated into the wider community. This sort of thing makes depressing reading, but the onus is on the immigrant population to "get out more". Whatever visitors might think about the British character, which is naturally reserved, or even British foreign policy, they should remember that they are the visitors here and that no one asked them to come. So they

Portrait of my mother.

*The original family home
in Sunel.*

The extended Noon family at the Bhawani Mundi bungalow.

Being knighted at Buckingham Palace.

Outside Buckingham Palace on the day of my investiture as Knight Bachelor (2002).

Dinner hosted by the Suterwalla brothers to celebrate my knighthood. l to r: Mansoor, Iqbal, Siraj, GN, Mohini, Hatim and Fakhruddin.

With Mohini at Buckingham Palace after receiving my knighthood. The portrait in the background is that of Queen Victoria.

With Her Majesty Queen Elizabeth II at the inauguration of the Memorial Gates. Next to the Queen is Baroness Shreela Flather.

GN with the King of Bahrain, His Majesty Shaikh Hamad Bin Isa Al Khalifa.

GN with daughters, sons-in-law and granddaughter. l to r: Zeenat and Arun Harnal, GN, Natania Harnal, Manraj and Zarmin Sekhon.

The Noon Hospital, Bhawani Mandi.

Residential accommodation for doctors and support staff.

GN with George Bush Snr. and His Highness Shaikh Khalifa Bin Salman Al Khalifa, Prime Minister of Bahrain.

His Holiness Shree Pramukh Swami, spiritual head of the Swaminarayam Sect (1994).

At the opening of Noon Products in 1995 with the Indian High Commissioner Dr Singhni, BaronessFlather, Sukhraj Nahar and the Bangladesh High Commissioner.

'Togged up' to receive an honorary
doctorate from Middlesex University –
one of five bestowed upon me by British
Universities.

In the London office with my
collection of 116 cricket bats.

The opening of the India Room, June 20th 2005. l to r: Paul Sheldon, GN, Sachin
Tendulkar, Sir John Major, David Stewart.

With Her Royal Highness The Duchess of Cornwall in my London office (March 2006).
l to r: Zarmin, Mohini, Arun, HRH, Manraj, GN, Zeenat.

With Prime Minister Tony Blair at his farewell dinner (2007).

Top: With Maharana Arvind Singh Ji Mewar and Mohini at the British Library, to inaugurate the digitised Mewar 'Ramayana', 15th May 2008.
Left: His Holiness Dr Mohammad Burhanuddin, spiritual leader of the Bohra community, with Prime Minister Gordon Brown and GN.

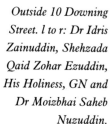

Outside 10 Downing Street. l to r: Dr Idris Zainuddin, Shehzada Qaid Zohar Ezuddin, His Holiness, GN and Dr Moizbhai Saheb Nuzuddin.

should leave their prejudices and preconceptions at home and be grateful for the extraordinary generosity of the British way of life.

It is up to Asian men in particular because, like it or not, the Asian way of life still represents a male-dominated society. They do not want to mingle with the host community so their lives revolve round their own kind and conversation always comes back to religion. This is the mentality even among the most educated in Asian society. I ask them: "Don't you have any British friends? You live in this country and yet you cocoon yourself away from the rest of the British population, watching Asian television." I recall one very learned speaker who knew the Koran by heart saying that it was better for a Muslim girl to marry a road-sweeper who is Muslim than to marry a rich man who is non-Muslim. That really disturbed me. How do you move on from a statement like that? You are insulting the country and all the people living here. You are insulting humanity. Who gave him the right to say these things?

I was born into a Muslim family, someone else was born into a Christian family – we had no choice. Who gives anyone the right to attack another religion? If non-Muslims are so despicable, why does God allow them to exist? Why is one religion right and another wrong? Who knows? My hope rests with the second and third generations who are different. Increasingly there are more inter-caste marriages and interaction with other cultures.

Statements promoting segregation are only harming Islam. The conspiracy theorists say that 9/11 was perpetrated by Jews. I met a qualified engineer who has lived in the US for most of his life who said that bombs were planted on each floor of the twin towers in New York by Jewish extremists and that these are what caused the disaster. Ridiculous. When I was growing up in Mumbai and Neil Armstrong walked on the moon, I heard a Muslim zealot in our street saying that it was all a Hollywood production stunt. If people do not want to believe, you cannot help them. If people have that mentality it is better to leave them to their own thoughts, but I am not prepared to ignore them if they are hurting other people, planting bombs or indoctrinating youngsters.

I do not know where it will end. Perhaps there will be some terrible event and people will say: "Enough – get rid of them all." America is very strict about this, and rightly so. In the mosques there, the language is much more moderate because the fanatics know that if they overstep the mark they will be picked up and deported. The UK should be in no doubt that it is a target. Pakistan and Egypt have both said that Britain is in effect harbouring, albeit unwittingly, terrorists or their supporters. If there is a rule about human rights that prevents their deportation, then change the rules. In any family, if there is one son who is a drug addict the father's duty is to reform him or report him because that son is disrupting the entire family. Similarly this country must not forget that it has to protect the lives of 69 million people, not just the civil rights of a few. When I talk to government ministers they all agree with me but they do not do anything because, I think, they feel trapped by the stranglehold of "PC" behaviour. That is the problem.

★ ★ ★

Just when you think that all the damage is being done by outspoken Muslim clerics, up pops Dr Rowan Williams, the Archbishop of Canterbury, who in February 2008 raised the prospect of aspects of Sharia law becoming acceptable in the UK. He said it was unavoidable that certain features of the Sharia system would become the norm in this country. His comments provoked protests from political and religious quarters alike, including some from Muslims.

The chairman of the Equality and Human Rights Commission, Trevor Phillips, described Dr Williams's comments as "muddled and unhelpful" and said that they would only succeed in fuelling anti-Muslim extremism. The Labour MP Khalid Mahmood was reported as saying: "I, along with the vast majority of UK Muslims, oppose any such move to introduce Sharia here. British law is the envy of the world." *The Sun* newspaper gave a typically blunt assessment: "It's easy to dismiss Archbishop of Canterbury Rowan Williams as a silly old goat. In fact he's a dangerous threat to our nation."

The Vatican itself weighed in shortly afterwards when the Roman Catholics' key man on Islamic relations, Cardinal Jean-Louis Tauran, president of the Vatican's Pontifical Council for Interreligious Dialogue, said: "I think it was a mistake, a mistake because, above all, one has to ask what type of Sharia. And then, it was a bit naïve." The Cardinal added: "One can understand his good intentions but it seems to me he did not take into consideration either them [the Muslims], the English juridical system, or the reality of Sharia."

Although I do not doubt that Dr Williams gave his words great thought, in my view his comments were at best ill-considered and at worst dangerous. I was delighted when a government spokesman said that "the Prime Minister believes British law should apply in this country, based on British values". And a spokesman for the Ministry of Justice was quoted as saying that Sharia law "has no jurisdiction in England and Wales. There is no intention to change this."

I recognise that Jewish, Roman Catholic and indeed those of all faiths have their points of view about many things from marriage, abortion and divorce to contractual and financial matters, and some even have their own "courts", but whatever their feelings or rulings they all must obey the law of the land. The ideas Dr Williams was advocating amount to the thin end of a very nasty wedge. How long would it be before policemen were prevented from doing their duty because they might transgress some aspect of Sharia law?

The Archbishop only succeeded in upsetting everyone. Rational Muslims do not want Sharia law here. How can people in authority or positions of influence even think about it? How can you have two laws in one land? Some even suggest that King Abdullah in Saudi Arabia wants to move away from these old ideas but cannot because of powerful religious bodies. At least he has apparently realised that the world has moved on. Yet what are we doing in the UK? We are trying to go backwards.

Let me give an exact, commercial parallel. When I started my company, Noon Products, I had success because, among other things, I was offering straightforward, authentic Indian food. The best thing is to go in a straight line. Indian food is Indian food; Italian food is Italian food. In your home you can bastardise it but not in public. It is exactly the same with trying to recognise bits of foreign laws in Britain. The government should make it crystal clear that it wants residents to adopt British ways and not try to have a bit of this and a bit of that. The British are plain speakers, and they like clarity.

Sharia law was devised 1400 years ago and in those days it was a different world. Populations were smaller; people knew little about other countries and what went on in them. To think that you can impose these same ideas in a mobile world where there are more planes flying in the sky than there are trains on the ground is nonsense. You have to accept the reality of life. If a Muslim says he wants to worship in the strict and true way then let him ride a camel, because the Prophet rode on a camel and not in a Cadillac. Some people just do what is convenient to them, selecting the bits that suit them. Their children are studying at British and American universities while the rest of the downtrodden and poor go to madrassas. That is Islam à la carte. I take my lead from Sarfraz Ahmad Shah, I call him Shah Saheb. He looks like any person you would pass on the street but he is a man of God with decades of spiritual practice behind him. Since he is an infrequent visitor to the UK, normally living in Pakistan, I take every opportunity to visit him with Mohini. He is a wise man and a good advisor.

If Muslim people want Sharia laws I would tell them to go to countries like Saudi Arabia where they would be more comfortable. That is not to criticise Saudi Arabia – they have their traditions and their laws too – but you can go and live there if you wish to follow the strict style of Islamic observance. In short, if you come to my house and spend the weekend with me, I want you to follow my rules. If I say please don't smoke, then don't smoke; if I say please don't drink, then don't drink. You came to Great Britain of your own free will. You wanted to better yourself and educate your children. Fantastic. But make sure you live by the norms of this country and do not try to impose your will on your hosts.

There is nothing to stop any law-abiding British citizen from achieving anything. I am not convinced by talk of "glass ceilings" preventing immigrants from reaching their goals in Britain, where I would say there is generally a benign business environment that encourages people with the determination and energy to succeed. But just as I write these thoughts, the government under Gordon Brown's management scores a spectacular own goal with moves to tax non-domiciles an additional £30,000 a year. I will return to the direction in which I believe Britain is heading a little later, but suffice it to say for now that such short-sighted measures will only succeed in driving out the best of the crop of successful businessmen.

I was flattered to have been named in various lists of influential Muslims in Britain, but what is impressive is that the compilers of those lists, such as the "Power 100", have many thousands from which to choose – lords and ladies, sporting icons, academics and lawyers. There are names that all Britons would be familiar with such as those of Imran Khan, the cricketer turned politician, Amir Khan, the boxer, and Mohammed al Fayed, the boss of Harrods, as well as many distinguished politicians and businessmen and women whose names might not be so well known to the man on the Clapham omnibus!

The problem is that everyone wants to come to Britain because everything is free here, and it attracts good and bad apples alike. Almost the moment some of them arrive at the airport they apply for housing benefit and healthcare and education. I sometimes think that such generosity is ridiculous and it is little wonder that the country is so attractive to people, whatever their motives. Newcomers are given three- and four-bedroom houses almost the day they walk through immigration control. You cannot let people be parasites. They should work for what they are given and many of them do. The National Health Service is said to be creaking under the strain of so many new immigrant patients but that has to be balanced with the fact that without immigrant workers the NHS itself would cease to function. What I object to is a man staying at home for ten years and doing nothing to contribute to society – perhaps even having lots of children, who in turn become a burden. In these cases you have got to put a stop to such largesse.

Someone, some country, some leader, has to show the way, and not for the first time in history France has stood alone in her robust attitude to those who threaten her. On 8 June 2007 I wrote an article in the *Financial Times* on the issue of civil liberties and the meaning of real democracy. I argued that terrorists were using these concepts as a shield behind which they could hide while at the same time they were plotting to kill us. Quite simply, I felt that the scales of justice had been tilted too far against the law-abiding citizen in Britain and that the balance should be restored.

I wrote that we should take a leaf out of the French book and consider the policy that was being vigorously pursued by that country's new President, Nicholas Sarkozy. As an immigrant himself, M. Sarkozy was uncompromising about how people who plotted against their country of residence should be treated: if found guilty, they should be deported. He made it clear that France would not tolerate extremist preachers and he proposed state funding to stop foreign extremists from indoctrinating Muslim communities. I quoted some facts at the time: Islamist terrorists had not attacked France since 1995; meanwhile Britain had foiled thirty-three such plots in the years leading up to 2007. It was time, I felt, for Britain to adopt France's policy of zero tolerance.

How can we live with a situation where the security services believe there are 400,000 people in the UK sympathetic to so-called violent jihad and saying they are doing this in the name of my religion? Of those 400,000, the police think that more than 1000 are Islamic activists. If by that they mean plainly and simply that they want to murder other British citizens then these people do not belong here and they have forfeited their rights.

The debate rages about how long we can detain suspects. Well, we must be guided by the experts on this matter. We have perhaps the finest judiciary in the world and a police force second to none – I am happy to follow their advice. Yes, we have to be careful to strike the right balance between civil liberties and law and order, but at the moment the blind pursuit of civil liberties and human rights, not to mention the political correctness I have already referred to, has done nothing but harm to the reputation of my religion. Be in no doubt – most right-thinking Muslims would welcome a change of approach by the government.

This is a cross-party matter and one in which opposition MPs should do everything they can to support strong and decisive action by government. The security forces need all the backing – financial and in terms of personnel – they can get to meet this challenge. I do not mind the police attending any mosque to listen to what is being said. What have I or the preachers to fear? If the imams stick to the teaching of the Koran they should welcome all comers. What have they got to hide?

I hope the decision to split the British Home Office into two separate departments, for security and justice, in 2007 has the desired effect: more focused action against today's real threats. I fear that we might simply be rearranging the desks and not tackling the real weakness, which is the lack of will to eradicate the threat in our midst, and to do it before the next attack, without vacillating or hesitating and wondering how it will play on the TV news channels up against the civil rights lobby.

When I wrote my article back in June 2007 I questioned the wisdom of dropping the term "war on terror" because I saw it then and see it still as a war. It is certainly a fight, and I think we are all agreed on calling the perpetrators of this evil what they are – cowards, bullies and murderers.

I have been critical of British methods only because I love the country so much. The rest of the world has also got to be on its guard against religious bigotry – it is a global problem. My motherland, India, is not immune. When Salman Khan, star of more than fifty movies, unveiled a wax statue of himself in Madam Tussaud's in London and described it as an honour, he could scarcely have expected the reaction he got. Within moments, it seemed, Mufti Salim Ahmad Qasmi, a Muslim cleric in India, said the statue was illegal according to the Sharia law, which forbids depictions of all living creatures and issued a fatwa against Salman Khan for allowing Madame Tussaud's to make a statue of him because it was sinful. Who on earth is this cleric to dictate such nonsense?

The same sort of thing happened to Sania Mirza, the young Indian female tennis star who became the first Indian woman to reach the fourth round of a Grand Slam at the US Open. I am proud of her, of what she has achieved and what she has done for her country. Even though she may be some forty years younger than I am, I will salute her when I meet her. But some cleric issued a fatwa of his own, in effect ordering her to cover up, to stop wearing short skirts. Is she supposed to wear a hijab or a Burkha and run around the court in that?

We have all got to find a way to live together. Integration is irreversible, and given time there will be greater acceptance even if there are occasional flare-ups. Beneath our skin we are all the same, but it seems that man is destined to fight with his neighbour, even his own family, at the slightest provocation.

I was happy to join a new organisation in 2006 called the Coexistence Trust, which brings Muslim and Jewish political leaders together to fight against increasing Islamophobia and anti-Semitism worldwide. It was founded by Prince Hassan bin Talal of Jordan and Lord Janner of Braunstone. As our website states, the Trust seeks to build a unique bridge to intervene at a senior political level whenever and wherever there are racist attacks against Muslims or Jews. Membership of the Trust has spread within a short time to include leaders in almost forty countries.

What can be done about the never-ending conflict between Jew and Arab in the Middle East? We have all seen atrocities committed in Palestine and Israel. I have been to Tel Aviv and I have been to Palestine. The first mistake in trying to resolve this conflict is to apportion blame, so let us not say who is right and who is wrong. If we follow that path we will never find peace.

Other conflicts in the world have been settled: World War I was settled, World War II was settled, the split between East and West Berlin was overcome. The Middle East crisis is not being settled because both sides are taking an egoistic approach. "I am not going to give in – you give in." "No, you give in first." No one wants to be the first to lay down their weapons because they feel it will be regarded as surrender and humiliation. But rather than a sign of weakness, I would argue that it would be a sign of strength. Of course there has to be equality. Today if you go to Tel Aviv you will see that it is a very prosperous city; Israel is a prosperous country. If I took someone blindfolded to Tel Aviv they would think they were in America when they heard all the sounds of a bustling city. By contrast, in Palestine there is such poverty. People are living in a single room – sometimes two or three families together. There is no privacy, no chance of intimacy. There is squalor and hunger. There is a terrible harshness that one day will have to come to an end.

As I have mentioned, I have been called upon to arbitrate on many occasions in both India and the UK, perhaps where two brothers are arguing over the direction or division of the family business, or on some other issue where the parties have become deadlocked. On all these occasion I have managed to settle the matter successfully on the principle of logic, not on the principle of wealth – and for "wealth" you can read "power". Every human being has an ego, and unless every human being is prepared to harness his ego you will always have conflict. But the world is not a bad place even though once in a while you come across an individual who cannot be persuaded to do what is best for everyone.

In the Middle East, Israel is the powerful side; it is a subsidiary, if you like, of America. That is not a crime – it is simply a fact of life. If I were sitting alone in a room and twenty people burst in and threatened me, I would not fight. I would say, "Let's negotiate." Palestinians must realise that they are fighting a giant that they will not defeat by force of arms so they must find an alternative, more creative and positive strategy. At the same time, I would say to the Israelis: "You have all the might – why are you crushing these people? They are already destroyed. Now is the time to show compassion."

One has to go to Palestine to see the plight of people. There is no dignity left. If you go to Tel Aviv you see incredible prosperity because it is bankrolled by America. So in my view the obligation is on Israel to "give in first" precisely because it is more powerful. If Palestine wants 10 per cent of the territory then Israel should give 15 per cent, and Palestine must realise the fact that it cannot beat an invincible foe. The story of David and Goliath is not played out every day. Yes, this would be a politically unpopular move in Israel, but the Prime Minister must take the people into his confidence first and ask them how many children they are prepared to lose. Do they want to fight all of their lives? Don't they want peace in their lifetime?

There have to be conditions, of course. They should not allow outsiders like Syria to interfere, for example. When you have a fight with your neighbour, you are the person affected, not the person looking on from across the street. He is only supporting one side or the other because he is at a safe distance and is unaffected. So who is losing out here? The ordinary Palestinian and the ordinary Israeli – no one else.

The argument is over temples and churches, which are bricks and mortar, no matter how revered. The most unfortunate part is that historically these religions all stem from the same source – the Abrahamic religions. The foundation of the Judaeo-Christian-Muslim line of religions began with a man named Abraham in about 2000 BC. The Koran speaks of the Prophet Jesus and the Prophet Moses and it says "Peace be upon them". If that exalted position is given to them in the Koran, what are we fighting for? These are all manmade arguments.

Yasser Arafat, as Chairman of the Palestinian Authority, fought for many years. The whole world knows how corrupt he was, and there was never going to be peace in his lifetime for the simple reason that if there were peace all the aid would be regulated properly; there would be Prime Ministers and Presidents and proper governance, and his "shop" would have to shut. In July 2000, at the Middle East Peace Summit at Camp David, US President Bill Clinton managed to get Chairman Arafat and the Israeli Prime Minister, Ehud Barak, to meet. A peace agreement was tantalisingly close because Barak had gone out on a limb and made concessions, much to the fury of many of his own people. But Arafat refused to accept the deal and a golden opportunity was missed.

One day a deal will be done. I always said to politicians that as long as Arafat was alive there would no chance of peace, but now there is a chance because they are talking and there is a democratic government in Palestine. However, even the Palestinians are fighting among themselves. You have the two Palestinian factions, Hamas and Fatah, in bitter and bloody conflict – why? The answer is simple. The conflict is driven by political ambition. Individuals are using Palestine for their own ends. If Palestine becomes a stable country, both will want power.

When you negotiate with someone it is always "give and take", to use a well-worn cliché, and I say this as someone of Indian origin, from a country with its own civil war. One day the Kashmiri issue will be settled between India and Pakistan. There have been two wars, in 1965 and 1999, and many lives have been lost. Still there is tension, but logic tells me that the Kashmiri question will be resolved. Who ever thought that the Berlin wall would come down or that the Soviet Union would disintegrate and all its republics become countries? Gorbachev saw the reality of the situation. The USSR has been dismantled on the basis of logic. I would give credit to Vladimir Putin, who stepped down as President in 2008 to become Prime

Minister, for one thing: he took control of a country that was in danger of being overrun by nothing more than gangsters. Russia could have gone to pieces. Boris Yeltsin, who ended up an alcoholic, in my view took the right decision when, as the new millennium dawned, he resigned and handed over power to Putin. But now the fledgling democracy is under threat, with the 2008 elections widely dismissed by observers as a sham orchestrated by Putin.

In politics you have to realise that your friends are never your friends for life. Your friends will use you and some may later dump you, but that is just the way it is. The West was more than happy to support Saddam Hussein of Iraq in his eight-year war against Iran. Now that war is forgotten for the time being. President Mahmoud Ahmadinejad was fêted in March 2008 when he went to Baghdad for the first official state visit by an Iranian leader to Iraq since 1979.

You cannot suppress people all your life; you cannot even suppress your children all your life. Take Pakistan. Because Russia was very active and always defying the USA, Washington had to handle Pakistan with kid gloves because it was the nearest country to Russia. And of course we know the history. The Russians went into Afghanistan and the USA supported the Mujahideen, and one Osama bin Laden, to drive out the Russians. Bin Laden later turned against America and succeeded in uniting disparate terrorists groups under the umbrella of al-Qaeda. So no one in politics is a friend forever: they all use you, and the bigger the power, the bigger the users.

I became a Trustee of the Maimonides Foundation, which also promotes Jewish-Muslim dialogue. I wish there were no need for such organisations, but it is not just Muslims and Jews who are fighting one another. Even within a country like Kenya – for so many years Africa's shining example to the rest of the continent – people of the same nation and the same racial background started killing each other, fighting over disputed elections. In this case it was tribal conflict, where neighbours who had been living together for many years suddenly become sworn enemies. At the root of it was not racism but the old sins of greed and envy. One group that had been in power for a long time did not want to give up their position, while another

159

group felt that they had been cheated out of their right to govern. Both sides stooped to anything, even murder, to achieve their ends.

As in all conflicts, it is the innocent and the poor who suffer the most. My time as a board member of CARE International UK taught me so much about the suffering of the people at the bottom of the "food chain". CARE helps 48 million poor people in some seventy countries every year to try to escape from poverty. It says a great deal about society if people in the twenty-first century are reduced to picking up bows and arrows as they did in Kenya to settle their scores. Ultimately wars are started because of the egos of the rulers. They never ask permission of the public, although so often wars are said to be in their name. The powerful remain protected and well fed while the civilians suffer the consequences.

Zimbabwe is a classic example where the ruler has governed by force of arms, living in sumptuous style while his people starve and hyperinflation is soaring at over 1000 per cent. Officially organised rallies proclaim their adoration of Robert Mugabe, but the day when he dies those same people who were supporting him will say what a tyrant he was and thank God that he is gone. Saddam Hussein, Hitler, Mugabe – the only govern through the terror in the hearts of their people.

As I suggested at the start of this chapter, the key to all understanding is education. Education means not being afraid to discuss, debate and even argue about events, and most importantly it is about learning from history, even that part of history that some might regard as painful. I joined with some fifty other Asians in February 2007 in an initiative to encourage youngsters to learn more about the British Empire. It is an intrinsic part of Indian history and people who come to live here should know about the past as it will help them understand what being British is all about. No one pretends the British Empire was without its faults, but equally we cannot pretend that it did not exist.

If taught with honesty and in the spirit of exploration, history can explain so much and should unite, not divide. But we have to be prepared to study and learn with an open mind clear of prejudice and envy, free of harboured grudges about distant wrongs, and with a willingness to build for a common good.

Chapter Sixteen

THE BOHRA COMMUNITY – REASON IN A CHANGING WORLD

Perhaps thinking of a common good is the right way to begin what I regard as a special chapter. I am a member of the Bohra sect: Shia Muslims hailing from the Yemen but now based in India. We believe that His Holiness Al-Dai Al-Fatimi, Dr Syedna Mohammed Burhanuddin, who became our fifty-second spiritual and temporal leader in 1965, follows a direct line of succession stretching back to the Prophet Mohammed (*pbuh*). It is an article of faith of the Dawoodi Bohras that such an imam would always be alive on earth to continue the teaching. There are one million followers throughout the world and some 4000 in Great Britain. In all probability most readers will never have heard of us. We are a relatively small sect but also we are peaceful; if you are quiet, you pass unnoticed. It is possible to be a Muslim without wanting to take over the world!

When I was a boy and my father was still alive, His Holiness's father used to visit Sunel and would stay at our house, bringing his son, the present Syedna, with him. His son was a young man at the time and I just a child, but I was fortunate to have been able to grow up as it were knowing him all this time. It was an incredible honour and a privilege to think that such a holy man would even visit us. But we were also fortunate to have a big enough house to accommodate him and his entourage, and I imagine he felt comfortable staying there. I remember long evenings listening to him and my mother, who was very outspoken, respectfully arguing the issues of the day. This, of course, was before my father and elder brother fell ill and the business suffered, reducing us to living in a one-room flat in Mumbai.

Bohras have an exceptional admiration for His Holiness, going way beyond what many would regard as normal reverence – even to the point of kissing his car. I suppose it is the equivalent of the followers of Christ in the Bible stories believing that just touching the hem of his cloak would bring blessings. Such is the zeal and loyalty the Bohras have to their faith and His Holiness Syedna. He is not aloof or remote from his million followers. He is approachable, and I am sure would want to spend time with each and every one of them if he could. But he travels the globe, even though he is now in his nineties, setting out from his base in Mumbai, giving advice and guidance, pointing the faithful in the right direction, all in a very down-to-earth manner, treating world leaders and shopkeepers with the same respect. It is a special gift that has an extraordinary impact on all who meet him. If he doesn't know the answer to a particular difficulty he will ask one of his people to find out. It is said that a piece of paper or file never remains on his desk for more than twenty-four hours without being dealt with – I wish I could say the same about myself!

One of the finest gifts His Holiness Syedna has given our community is to steer us away from any form of extremism. Nothing could be timelier as the whole world struggles to cope with indiscriminate threats. I doubt whether more than a handful of Bohras have been sent to jail as petty thieves. Certainly not a single one has been convicted as a terrorist or terrorist sympathiser. The shame of having their name reported, not in a newspaper but to His Holiness, would be unbearable. He is certainly strict, but in a mild way. I would say, rather, that he is firm, always giving a strong emphasis to education. We are proud of our reputation for having well-educated boys and girls – there is absolutely no distinction – and most of them graduate from university. Both His Holiness and his father before him have been passionate about education, regardless of sex.

We are also proud of our activity in business life. This is hardly surprising, as the word "Bohra" comes from the Gujarati word for a trader, and the name was given to us because originally we came predominantly from the trading and commercial communities. Like all religions, ours is evolving as the world around us changes. These can be difficult times, and there are pressures on our faith as on every other faith to introduce reforms to cope with various influences. We believe that the best way of doing this is through internal discussion rather than public debate and, perhaps for that reason, we are not well known outside our own community. Previous imams even withdrew into complete seclusion from the outside world, providing guidance to the faithful through their *dais*, who passed on the knowledge handed down to them from the imam. For more than four centuries twenty-three *dais* worked from their mountain bases in Yemen, where they lived to escape persecuting regimes.

The success of any grouping – be it a business, a faith or, dare I say it, a political party – lies in having the right leader. It is no different for our Bohra sect, and although we wish His Holiness long life, he is in his nineties and everyone is anxious to know whom he will appoint as his successor. He himself was chosen at a relatively young age, but so far His Holiness is keeping his thoughts on the subject of the succession to himself. He is a wise man, and in due course his decision will be revealed. Despite his years, he is a man of the modern age; he has met the world leaders. He has been awarded doctorates from seven world-renowned universities including the Al-Azhar, Cairo. He is well aware of the challenges that modern life will present to his successor; for example he has established a form of interest free loan (*Karzane Hasanat*) under Islamic Law to enable the community to escape the trap of not allowing money to be borrowed from financial institutions with the payment of interest.

He can draw on the knowledge he learned at the feet of his father and his own great wisdom that he has acquired from a lifetime of study and prayer. His choice will be a wise one: a man capable of handling the jet-age world of real globalisation and yet a man steeped in learning and spirituality.

In short I would say the Bohras are a well-regulated community. When someone says that he is a Bohra, the response is invariably: "He must be a good and honest man." That is the impression created because we are never involved in anything underhand, for which I give all the credit to His Holiness. He gave one instruction in particular to his followers that is especially relevant in today's highly mobile world. He has always said that wherever you live you must be loyal to that country. There is no instruction to subvert the religion, education or behaviour of the host nation, and no rule that says you must convert everyone you meet to Islam.

I have a great relationship with His Holiness, his elder son, Shahzada Qaid Zohar Ezuddin, and indeed the rest of the family. I was deeply honoured when His Holiness's son said on one occasion at a large gathering, "Gulam Noon is my friend." I am a very lucky man that he should have singled me out in that fashion. Perhaps it makes up for all my other spiritual shortcomings! I was particularly honoured when in 2001 His Holiness awarded me the NDI, the most prestigious title for those who have made a major contribution to the Bohra community and it was formally presented by his son, Shahzada Qaid.

I remember that it was my good fortune to be able to play a small but important role in His Holiness's life. About three or four years ago I had been received by His Holiness and blessed by him. I was in a marvellous mood and had gone out for dinner, returning home shortly after midnight. I got a call from our London Amil (priest), Dr Idris Bhaisaheb Zainuddin, to say that His Holiness's wife, affectionately known as Busahaiba, had passed away. I rushed back to Southall and we met at my factory. Dr Idris explained that her dying wish was that she should be buried in the grounds of our Northolt mosque residential complex, which was an almost impossible request as a body cannot normally be buried in a residential area. I said that this was a tall order but I would do my best. So at two in the morning I knocked on the door of the Mayor of Ealing. I knew him well, and he was very understanding. I told him that I was now asking for a big favour. I needed him to use his influence and, with the assistance of the Chief Executive of Ealing Council, get permission for her body could be buried according to her wishes. Happily, her wish was granted.

Shortly after that, when I paid a condolence visit to His Holiness, he took the microphone and said to me in front of the congregation: "I am extremely grateful for what you did." If I have achieved nothing else I am proud to be able to say that every Bohra in the world knows that I was able to provide that small service and help my community in that way.

My relationship with His Holiness and his family is one based on understanding and considerable indulgence on their part because in many respects I cannot reach the ideals laid down in the Bohra teaching, particularly with regard to business. I know I am not the perfect Bohra, but I have always tried to conduct myself with the greatest integrity. No one can say that I have borrowed £5 or £5 million and not repaid it. I have my ethics and standards for my business as well as my personal life that have come naturally to me. It is impossible always to follow the letter of the religious law – if we could we would all be saints.

I suppose it is a question of belief. I would like to think I am trying to be a good Muslim and good Bohra. I have tremendous respect for the Bohra community as a whole and I believe it is a wonderful sect. I abide by most of the rules most of the time. I will always work for the community and obviously we will help each other, but I think that applies within every community. The most important thing to stress about the Bohra is that there is no radicalism among us, and wherever we live we must remain loyal to the country: this is the message that His Holiness consistently preaches.

Not everyone follows their faith to the last degree but that does not make them any less worthy. It behoves us all to respect those whom we meet, just as it is our duty to respect the country in which we live and its traditions. It is hardly a difficult task, and it is a formula for success in business life as well as personal life. No one is asking you to agree with every word someone utters, or indeed to agree with every custom of a land, but we are all obliged to allow people to hold their own views and follow their own traditions.

Crucially we must keep the dialogue between all peoples and all faiths going. I was thrilled when the Prime Minister, Gordon Brown, acceded to my request to meet His Holiness, Syedna Mohammed Burhanuddin, on 16th May 2008. I took His Holiness, his eldest son, his UK representative and his son-in-law to 10 Downing Street. The Prime Minister welcomed Syedna with a beaming smile said how delighted he was to meet him. Syedna, just as happy to have the opportunity to see Gordon Brown, promised to pray for him and his family. Syedna's son, Shahzada Qaid Zohar, kindly said I was the leader of the Bohra community to which Gordon

Brown replied with a laugh that I was a leader of all communities. After an exchange of gifts we left. I was delighted with the meeting and for the Prime Minister to have met such a holy man. But the serious point is that such meetings between religious and political leaders can only bring greater understanding.

Chapter Seventeen

On Politics, Business and Immigration

In the summer of 2007 I received a call from Downing Street asking me to attend a private meeting with the Prime Minister. So on Wednesday, 1 August 2007, once again I found myself walking through that famous door. The mood had changed: there was of course a new Prime Minister by then. "Not flash, just Gordon" was the catchy phrase ad agency Saatchi & Saatchi came up with to mark the change of style.[1]

The very morning Gordon Brown returned from his first trip to the United States as Prime Minister I sat alone with him in the garden of No 10 enjoying the sunshine and chatting about a lot of issues but particularly about education and extremism. I would give my views and opinions as honestly and as bluntly as I have done throughout my life.

I will respect the confidentiality of the detail of what Gordon Brown said to me because, as I write this, he is still Prime Minister, but I would say we covered a great deal of ground and I hope my thoughts were of some value to him. I was touched and humbled when he began by apologising profusely for the adverse publicity I had received over the Cash for Honours saga.

To be Prime Minister of any country must be a daunting task, no matter

---

[1] Saatchi &Saatchi was Margaret Thatcher's favourite agency and was credited with helping the Conservatives win the 1979 general election with the slogan "Labour isn't working".

how much one has longed for the job, but to be Prime Minister of Great Britain in 2007/08 was a mighty challenge. The financial climate was looking bleak and, very shortly, due to get a great deal worse. We seemed to be trapped in the Iraqi conflict with no easy way out. There were attempted terrorist attacks, flooding and the return of foot and mouth disease. All that in his first 100 days in the job! He knew I had written and spoken extensively on the threat of Muslim extremism. I was flattered when he asked if he could quote from my articles in his own speeches. I sent him copies of all the articles later.

As a businessman, I was directly affected by the policies of Gordon Brown as Chancellor. For an entire decade he wisely steered the British economy, keeping it buoyant and in good shape even whilst our neighbours on the Continent suffered economically at various times. He was a safe pair of hands and that is what is needed in a prime minister. That morning in Downing Street he was also a kind and charming host and I was ready to do my bit if called upon.

I am a New Labourite so I was disappointed by the direction events seemed to be taking early in 2008. Obviously, as an entrepreneurial British Indian I find economics is close to my heart, and as an immigrant the handling of the non-domicile issue, which I touched on earlier, rang alarm bells for me, as it did for many of my friends. The new Chancellor, Alistair Darling, let it be known in his Pre-Budget Report (PBR) that "non-doms", as they are known, would have to pay an extra £30,000 a year on top of their taxes and there were suggestions that gains and income from assets kept offshore might also be of interest to the Her Majesty's Revenue & Customs. It seemed to be an off-the-cuff, knee-jerk idea that had not been properly thought through. We needed clarity and we were told we would not get that clarification until April. In the opinion of many of my non-dom friends, that was not good enough. It became the major talking point at every gathering, and I know that within days of the Pre-Budget Report at least three of my friends had started making arrangements to leave the country and had bought properties in Dubai. Another reason investments were flowing into Dubai and Bahrain was precisely that certainty to which I referred earlier. India is another example because people have confidence in the Prime Minister, Manmohan Singh, who is an economist as well as a politician; his focus is on ensuring that the country is run efficiently from both a political as well as an economic point of view. So I am baffled by the thinking that would even consider such a tax. The government rightly courts the business community. They talk to the business community, but they don't listen. No one is blessed with the ability always to be right, so when mistakes such as this are made people should not be too proud to climb down and admit they have got it wrong.

Eventually, when he came to deliver his first Budget on 12 March, the Chancellor of the Exchequer, Alistair Darling went ahead with his plan to impose the £30,000 a year charge on the estimated 100,000 to 200,000 people living in Britain who have financial interests abroad but do not pay UK taxes on those assets. Pressure and advice from business representatives to abandon the idea were ignored, although the lobbying did lift the threat to offshore assets. Possibly in a bid to reassure these people that the figure would not be hiked up again in future budgets, Darling said there would be no changes to the regime "in this Parliament or the next". His intention provided scant comfort.

This was not just a matter of a tax that to the vast majority of people being targeted would not have made much difference. Far more serious was the message it was sending out: "If you come here we will make you pay additional taxes." Or, to put it more bluntly: "We don't want your business." So what will people do? They will take their companies elsewhere. At least one estate agent was reported as saying that non-doms had been scaling back on property purchases since October 2007.

People are prepared to pay taxes up to a point, but if you squeeze too hard – "until the pips squeak", as they say – don't be surprised if the taxpayers move elsewhere. It happened in India, where we had such a strict regulatory system and tax regime that people left in droves and many, like me, came to the UK. But the Indian authorities saw the error of their ways and now capital gains tax has been lifted along with gift tax and death duties – indeed gradually the whole tax regime is becoming business-friendly. But what are we doing in the UK? We are creating a climate of uncertainty. Some thought that Gordon Brown was a tax maniac as

Chancellor, and that Darling, his successor, but without the independence of thought and movement of Brown, did not know what he was doing. The government had become a laughing stock in some people's eyes. It began to slump in the polls, and even in India people were shocked. The government seemed determined to shoot themselves in the foot at every opportunity.

The business community believed that the non-dom levy was just an unnecessary tax and that it was curbing our initiative and entrepreneurship. People love to come to this country because it is a cultured society and English-speaking. They will conduct their business and pay taxes, and the residue may well be taken out. In my case, when I sold my company for £50 million in 2000, I was advised by a leading accountancy firm that I would be able to take the entire amount out of the country because I was non-domiciled and I was born in India – provided I was prepared to live outside the country. But I decided not to do so. I had not earned this money to be self-exiled. I will pay my tax. And like any other company we pay full tax, PAYE, income tax, VAT – but please don't fine me as well!

I wonder if the government had analysed this properly, if at all. The money we take out soon comes back in through investments in the UK and, with more than one tax payer in most households, the £30,000 levy will be charged several times over in one family. We contribute to every aspect of community life, and for all of that the government imposes this punitive penalty. It is not acceptable. Sir Digby Jones, later Lord Jones and former head of the Confederation of British Industry, who was brought into Gordon Brown's "big tent" as Trade Minister,[2] spoke out passionately about this. He complained that he was charged with the role of selling Britain to the rest of the world yet no one had consulted him. Some months later in August 2008, he announced that he would stand down as Trade Minister.

Most of the Indians who have made it in the UK are non-doms. We graduated from shopkeeping to industry to financial institutions, and we

---

[2] When he was elected, Gordon Brown sought to recruit professionals and expert advisers from across the political sphere in his "Government of all the talents".

have built up our businesses over twenty years, not five. What attracted people is precisely the business-friendly environment. Suddenly the tables were being turned. My advice to Gordon Brown is to encourage, not squash, the entrepreneurial spirit that generates wealth and employment. Even if not a single non-dom leaves, what about the ones who are yet to arrive? They will now be having second thoughts about bringing their money to Britain. India and China are both waiting. The Irish are saying come here! And why not?

As the saying goes: "We must understand what we can get by what we can lose." In the non-dom situation, yes, the government will get £3 billion, but it could lose £30 billion. How many companies do they think will pull out or change their minds about coming in the first place? George Osborne, the shadow Chancellor, came up with the idea of a tax of £25,000, and less than a week later Labour seemed to think that they had to go one better ... or one worse. The simple fact of the matter is that non-domiciles create wealth for the UK, and even if they take money out they will bring it back later, perhaps to buy properties or to open other businesses. It is not as though the money is going out of the country for good and all.

Governments have to tread carefully in case they scare off investment money. That is not to say that they should be frightened of asking questions about where money is coming from or who is the ultimate beneficiary. But the world is a big place and there are plenty of other eager hands outstretched.

There is an unspoken agreement in Dubai that everyone can invest their funds there, as long as they don't cause any mischief. The money has come in large part from the rich Saudis and other Middle Eastern magnates who have withdrawn their money from America and had to find an alternative home for it. They saw what was happening in Dubai and they liked the style of the authorities. Dubai was marketed well. Bahrain is also an attractive option: it is small, but it enjoys good law and order and accountability, although I think it could be marketed more aggressively.

The point for the UK is that all these countries are competing for investors. They will ensure that their regimes are as favourable as possible. It is simple finance. The hard facts are that money will flow to the most favourable tax areas. And I am not just talking about that of foreign companies. Belatedly Alistair Darling was reported to have set up a working group to come up with plans to stop the exodus to Ireland of companies who are concerned not only about current taxation but also about threatened increased taxation on overseas earnings. A double whammy. People like Sir Martin Sorrell, chief executive of the mighty WPP advertising empire, which pays taxes in many different countries around the world, was said to be thinking about joining the likes of Shire Pharmaceuticals and United Business Media and moving WPP's tax domicile across the Irish Sea.

The real point is that while I believe London is still the financial capital of the world, I also believe that this is a very fragile position and it may only be for geographic convenience that many firms have a base, if not their main base, in the UK. It has been strongly argued that when times get hard the power players with the biggest financial clout – still the Americans for now – retreat home with their money to New York and the relative safety of Wall Street. But there is another dimension, called the "new Arabism", and the vast cash mountains built from rising oil revenues are being re-invested in their own countries, creating towering new buildings, hotels, leisure centres and shopping malls in Dubai and its other Gulf neighbours. This is not the time for Great Britain to start making financial enemies.

Before the Spring of 2008 was out, the government had slipped on another domestic financial banana skin when it had to do a U-turn over the abolition of the 10p tax band announced in Gordon Brown's last budget as Chancellor. His successor, Alistair Darling, was forced to announce a £2.7 billion handout to low and middle earners in what was effectively a mini budget to buy off a threatened backbench revolt. It all looked clumsy; the *Financial Times* said it was more like panic. The Tories called it a cynical bid to buy votes in a by-election at Crewe and Nantwich in May. It didn't work. The Conservatives won their first by-election against Labour in thirty years, turning a 7000 vote deficit into an almost 8000 vote majority.

But all of this soon was forgotten when the débâcle of the September financial crash hit and we witnessed the collapse of some of the best known banking names around the world, triggered by excesses on Wall Street. As

172

confidence in the banking system evaporated, no country was immune from the fallout including India. Could the UK have been better prepared? Should the Government have put money aside during the good times? Should Downing Street have curbed the climate of greed in London never mind what American bankers were doing?

All these questions were thrown at the Government but the real question was what should be done in the future? Clearly banks should not be so profligate, there should be greater oversight of their dealings and never again will mortgages be so cheap.

But this crisis had yet to strike as we sat in the garden in Downing Street where one of the dominant topics of conversation, which will remain long after the financial horrors are resolved, was naturally enough immigration and integration. Britain is a pluralistic society and has rightly, in my view, welcomed immigrants who have been prepared to do the work that indigenous Britons were only too happy to hand over. If we did not have immigrants, many of our businesses and much of our basic infrastructure would suffer; our transport system and the NHS would be struggling. But now we have all these people and we have to consider how many more the UK can take. We can only accommodate so many. If the room will only hold ten people, hold a meeting for ten people and not twenty. It is simple logic. We have a mature society and democracy in Britain, but there is always a danger that for the sake of political correctness, or a party's political advantage with a new vote-catching idea, we find ourselves filling up the country with too many immigrants who will disturb the balance and upset the people – particularly the young people – of the host community. I do not want youngsters to think that the Poles, Indians, Pakistanis or Somalis have taken their jobs. That cannot be allowed to happen, although I fear to an extent it already has. The double irony is that the Poles and other East Europeans have started giving the jobs back and leaving for more favourable economic climes. The falling value of the pound in the Spring of 2008 meant Britain was no longer the big draw, and this has left some sectors – fruit-picking, building, hotels and catering, for example – struggling to find workers for the vineyards, so to speak.

Bluntly, I think we are self-sufficient now. We should wait for five or ten years, and until all the newcomers have been properly integrated and assimilated into the country. Until then we should just shut the door. The UK is so attractive from almost every point of view that everyone wants to come. I can already hear howls of protest and claims that we are now part of a greater Europe, and that such a strategy would be against the rules. Well, we have a say in the European Council, so we should fight to change the rules and for the right to close our doors. France and Germany are much bigger countries and they have room. We should be logical about this and decide which country can best accommodate the many thousands who understandably want to improve their lot and the lot of their families. The British population, in my opinion, is large enough and we should switch the focus to ensuring that everyone has a job, which is essential both to the economy and to give them their dignity. Once they have, they will work for the good of the country. Today some of them are just getting the dole and free houses for doing nothing. We have made them parasites when we should be making them proud of being British and being respected for the work they do.

Assuming that we cannot shut our doors, I would say now to any potential immigrant that when you come here you must respect the law of the land and try to understand its culture, no matter how baffling you may find it at first. No one will ask you to change your religion, but do not expect everyone else to agree with yours – there is room for all religions in this life, and who is to say that any of us have got it right? You have not received a personal invitation from the Queen to come to the UK, so if you do not like the customs of her people, you are free to leave. If, however, you choose to stay and one day you step out of line, expect to be sent to prison or to be deported.

Incidentally, I hope that the regime in prisons will get tougher. According to recent reports, life is so cushy that none of the inmates wants to leave, let alone escape. Drug dealers are even said to be breaking into prisons to supply the demand! Criminals have forfeited the right to any special favours, rights or privileges. In prison, they should eat what everyone else eats, do what everyone else does, and if they have immigrated to the UK, at the end of their sentence they should be sent packing. Better still, deport them before they serve their time so that the burden of feeding and watering them does not fall on the British taxpayer. I read that some immigrants were actually being given a cheque to leave the country before their sentences were completed. I hope such an idea is not pursued because as soon as the criminals return home they will simply change their passports and be on the next plane back.

Despite the horrors of the financial market slump in March 2008, which seemed to paint the UK with the same brush as the US as sterling dropped out of favour, Britain is still a great country in which to do business. We should celebrate our achievements and our multiculturalism. Don't look immigrants with a critical eye, as if to say "What the hell are you doing here?" Instead, acknowledge their worth and the contribution they are making to society. I always told my managers to show respect to all the staff. Don't sit high up in your executive offices looking down on your workforce – be at their level and talk to them. Then you get better productivity. When I go to my plant I see the security people at the gate and wave hello. They are our front-of-house and are therefore important. On one occasion when I was driving away from work I saw a lady and gentleman walking home. So I stopped my car and said I knew they worked for my company, Bombay Halwa, and asked in which direction they were going. I dropped the woman at her bus stop and the man where he wanted to go. I do it all the time. It is just simple humanity and it creates goodwill – no doubt those two talked to twenty others. Cynics would say I did it for my own selfish motive, but I didn't think for one minute that this would be a clever PR stunt to please the workforce. If we can help one another, why not?

Not only is Britain a good country in which to do business, it is also a wonderful country in which to bring up a family and educate your children. We are privileged to have some of the greatest centres of learning in the world – whether we are talking about Eton or a comprehensive secondary school, Oxbridge or a college of further education, there is something for everyone. No one with the desire to learn will be deprived of an opportunity. Yes, of course, some have more opportunity than others, but I am convinced that sheer willpower and application will overcome every obstacle. Don't just complain about private education – I didn't have any sort of educational advantage. Apply yourself to your studies wherever you are at school and you will succeed. When I was daydreaming at my Central School in Mohammet Ali Road, Mumbai, I did not think how much better off I would be if I were studying at a private school. I was certainly dreaming, or should I say planning what I would become: I was inspired by the scenes of London I saw in my local cinema, but not jealous of the good fortune of the British. I wanted to improve myself and the fortunes of my family – that was the goal. When Idi Amin threw the Asians out of Uganda with little more than the clothes they stood up in, they were at rock bottom, but today many of those families are living in great comfort. So regardless of where you are on life's ladder, it is possible to climb up: you just need determination, grit and to make your own luck.

There was a time when an Indian's first destination for further education was Britain, but as I have said to many university Chancellors during my Presidency of the London Chamber of Commerce, many are now looking towards America. British universities should be as aggressive as American universities at marketing themselves in India and the Home Office should be more helpful to Indian students seeking student visas.

Sadly, what we see in many UK cities today is despair. When I arrived in London and marvelled at the people dancing in the street, they were celebrating a great victory in the World Cup. Now all they celebrate is getting through the week, and for that great achievement so many young people, including young professionals apparently stressed out by their work, are reduced to binge drinking. What has twenty-four-hour drinking brought this country but trouble, increased costs, dangers for the police and a general decline in morality? On top of the binge drinking there is obesity. Whatever happened to discipline and the ability to say "No more for me, thank you"? Why has the UK become the Fat Man of Europe? Great Britain has become Great Big Britain.

It boils down to simple courtesy and plain good manners. It is wrong as well as unhealthy to stuff your face with fast food, constantly grazing between meals, and it is equally wrong to drink so much in public that you lose control. In my childhood my parents said, after showing respect to us, that we should show the same respect to our elders, to our neighbours and above all to our teachers. Today teachers are mocked, beaten, knifed. Instead of being revered, teachers endure hideous pressures in school where it seems they can only take punishment and never dish it out when it is undoubtedly deserved. If I got a clip round the ear, I never forgot the error of my ways. Today teachers doing this would be taken to court by the malicious little tyrants who are bent on dragging the rest of their classmates down to their level.

Personally, I would bring back two years' military service – and that is not just an old fogey saying how much better it was in his day: in some ways it was and in some ways it wasn't. But I know from recent personal experience that national service works. Take a small country like Singapore where there is compulsory military or police service. I have a nephew there who was a typically boisterous and mischievous lad – perhaps a little too boisterous – and I worried about what might become of him. In due course he was drafted into the police and I was delighted to see the transformation in him a little while later. He had turned into what we oldies would call "a fine young man". His parents, of course, played their part, but I am sure the greatest influence was the two years he spent in the police service. Service instils discipline. Today parents are so busy that they don't have time to look after their children: rushing home late, unable to prepare proper meals or supervise homework. But let us not look for excuses. My brothers and sisters and I lived in a single room for a time and my mother had to bring us up alone, so I hope I will be forgiven if I find the excuses regularly trotted out in the UK– truly a land of plenty – about how difficult life is to be pretty lame.

It seems only a small step from hooliganism in the classroom to crime on the street, and Britain is not immune from the relentless wave of criminality that is afflicting every big city around the world. To let the punishment fit the crime is surely the only reasonable approach. Under Labour, many new laws have been passed – some would argue too many – and yet there is often no effective enforcement of the law. Nothing will be achieved until the police are allowed to do their job without the enfeebling restrictions that the politically correct lobby imposes on them. Human rights have overwhelmed the nation to such an extent that everyone is complaining about it. But do human rights only exist for the criminals? What about the victims? I have seen with my own eyes policemen being abused, and there is nothing they can do about it for fear of being sued. I have a great sympathy for the policemen and policewomen whom we are asking to swim in dangerous waters with their hands tied behind their backs.

Law is fear. Otherwise, you would need one policeman for every citizen. In India, in the village where I come from, if a policeman comes to your house it is considered terrible shame. In the UK, by contrast, some communities regard it as a joke, perhaps even a point of pride. Until the young hooligan and criminal element ceases to think of a spell in the police cells as a badge of honour, we will not be able to walk freely in our streets at night – or even in some places during the day, if we are the wrong colour. I do not want to see every policeman on the streets carrying a gun and I look forward to the day when men armed to the teeth with machine guns do not have to patrol our airports, but I do want to see the criminal classes tremble at the knock on their door. I am concerned about crime, not just as a private citizen but as a businessman. Crime eventually has an impact on all businesses, whether we are talking about the effects of petty vandalism, or the expense of stringent security measures or the issuing of ID cards. Everyone, it seems, has to have a criminal records check before they can be employed in even the most modest and innocent capacity. These are all costs that have to be met.

When I first came to Britain in the sixties no one seemed to have the worries that we all have today about being mugged in broad daylight or walking alone through public parks. Now you are constantly looking over your shoulder or wondering about the person standing next to you in a queue. All forms of public transport have become hazardous, particularly for the elderly, and air travel has become almost intolerable. If you are not put off by the personal checks on your body then you will probably be fearful about some of your fellow passengers.

Although statistically crime is falling in the UK, the impression we all have is that law and order is in decline; and, I have to say, the politicians are responsible for this. If you report someone suspicious to the police because you fear that they might be following you, the overburdened police will say that there is nothing they can do about it. They simply advise you

178

to call again if you are attacked, and no, don't take the law into your own hands. Once upon a time an Englishman's home was his castle, but today there is an open door policy. If I wait until I am attacked I might be dead, and if I defend myself I might be sued by the burglar. Is it too complicated to understand that if the burglar had not tried to break into my house in the first place I would not have had to use any force against him?

The police will make mistakes from time to time; they are only human and we all make mistakes in our professional and personal lives. Tragedies like the Jean Charles de Menezes shooting happen, and my heart goes out to the family.[3] But that sort of mistake is mercifully rare in the UK. When the police came to speak to me under caution during the Cash for Honours saga, they were so polite. I was amazed. They did not have to be, as I was a suspect in an investigation. I was very impressed. It is easy to snipe at the police when things go wrong, but for their very few mistakes, there are countless thousands of man-hours put in every year without blemish.

Of course, when the police do catch their suspects and they are finally brought before the courts, the magistrates and the judges have to be able to hand down meaningful sentences. If a criminal deserves to be sent to prison that is where he or she belongs. If there is no room in the prison then build another one. But I believe that if we made prison an unpleasant experience, rather than laying on TV and every other personal comfort imaginable, we would soon find the numbers of inmates declining. As a Justice of the Peace in India I knew that the sentences we gave were effective and it was rare to see repeat offenders before the bench. The judiciary do not pass the laws and they cannot be blamed when they are forced to release suspects if a case has not been made according to the letter of the law, or when sentencing guidelines are such that the punishment appears trivial for the offence. And that brings us back to the politicians. Good law is the answer, and legislation in the UK starts at Westminster.

The obvious next question is how good are our politicians. I am pleased to say that I live in a country where if I want to meet my local MP I can

---

[3] Jean Charles de Menezes was shot on 22nd July 2005 on the London Underground by police who mistook him for a potential suicide bomber.

knock on his or her door. We are blessed with a sound democratic process; after all, we have the Mother of all Parliaments. Gordon Brown wanted his Government of All the Talents, which is an excellent idea ... so long as their voices are heard and their counsel heeded!

As I sat with the Prime Minister in the garden I felt inspired by the very business-like approach he intended to bring to his leadership of the country. It was a different style from that of his predecessor, but it was workmanlike and highly intellectual. Although there is a lot on his plate, I remain very optimistic for my adopted country because, whichever political party is in charge, the resolute British common sense in the end seems to prevail. I still say it is the best country in the world in which to live, work and learn. There is of course always room for improvement, and so long as we recognise these lacunae in our society and we are prepared to address them, all will be well.

One thing we must accept is that, great as we are, we live on a small island and we cut ourselves off from our European neighbours at our peril. It is a peculiarly British characteristic not to want to belong to Europe. I understand the powerful sense of independence of the British people, celebrated in her anthem and hymns, but I am convinced that we must be part of Europe. I was a member of the committee of the Britain in Europe group so my colours are firmly fixed to the mast. If the USA had not become a confederation of all the states it would not have been so powerful. The American forefathers were wise enough to see that in unity they would survive and prosper. By combining the force of all the European countries we can make a difference. To be sure, we will have to make adjustments, and not everything will suit everyone, but by and large we will be productive members of the Union.

Nations are not made in one year but in fifty or a hundred. My grandchildren will think of themselves as European, not as English. I am all for Europe and, yes, there are certain things we will lose, certain things we will gain and certain things that will irk us and irritate. But in life not everything is always hunky-dory.

If we had a referendum on Europe today, in 2008, the vote would be against. A housewife sitting in Bradford would say: "I want my British passport, not a European one. I want my pound, not a euro." That is all part of the English wanting to be allowed to get on with their lives without outside interference. Brits don't like bureaucracy. I would not argue with that, but instead of burying our heads in the sand, I would say that if we do not like the way the European Court, for example, overrules us, we should just argue our case. We have a seat in the European Parliament so why not use our right to challenge and argue the point? Somewhere there will be a compromise.

Unless we consolidate we cannot have a mighty Europe, and a mighty Europe does not just mean France and Germany: it means all the small countries. Look at Ireland. People were leaving Ireland, but now, because of Europe, it is rejuvenated. People say the Irish bubble is about to burst, but it has not burst yet. I have been hearing the same thing about Dubai for twenty years and it is still going strong in 2008.

As I look back on the years I have spent in England, I remain a committed citizen without a shred of doubt about the wisdom of my decision, so long ago, to move my business and my family to the UK. I am also someone who, at this stage in his life, is able to reflect and to offer his time, seeking neither reward nor salary, after all I have served on many government advisory boards without looking at the financial gain. People like me speak our minds without fear or favour. Our advice is given honestly, without any agenda or "spin". We might be wrong, but at least we are speaking with the voice of experience.

I urge any government to focus on discipline and education. From these flow everything – prosperity, decency, law and order. If we have law and order, our Accident and Emergency hospitals will not have injured drunks filling the beds and out-patient departments every night and the NHS can instead spend its resources on the genuinely needy in state-of-the-art hospitals. If the hooligans and wannabe criminals in our classrooms become diligent students then the whole of our educational system will benefit, and so too will the youngsters themselves and their classmates.

Make use of the many successful businessmen and businesswomen in this country and put them to work advising us how better to run our health service, our transport, indeed all our infrastructure. These are the people who travel the globe and can bring insight and ideas from other cities. And we are not just European, we are global. Our financial systems are shaped by the global economy; the price of our bread is affected by the new demands for wheat from China; the value of our banks and the strength of our financial institutions are affected by decisions taken in other countries. All of these things make us part of the global community. I believe it is a tribute to the astonishing ingenuity, flexibility and individuality of the United Kingdom that we can rightly be called the financial centre of the world.

Now is not the time for us to become Little Englanders. There are new opportunities in China and the Far East. There are challenges nearer to home in an ever-expanding Europe. I would say now is the time to consolidate – to reassert our traditional values and be proud to be British.

Epilogue

For a moment, I shut myself off from the hubbub of the celebrations and tried to imagine what the same scenes must have been like exactly eighty years earlier. My father and my uncle would have felt the same sense of accomplishment, satisfaction and possibly even a little pride when their hospital opened in 1928. Later, with the support of a local maharajah, they had built a second one.

I am no maharajah, although Ram Giddomal, the successful entrepreneur and adviser to governments, humorously dubbed me and a number of others "the UK Maharajahs" is one of his books.[1] But I did insist on the finest quality for my own hospital. So here I was, back in my home town of Bhawani Mandi on 4 April 2008, enjoying the opening ceremony of my own Noon Hospital dedicated to the memory of my mother. Just as my father had insisted at his hospital, mine was open to all regardless of race, colour, creed or caste.

The hospital stands like a peacock in full plumage in the arid landscape of Rajasthan. "I saw it from the air and it looked like a palace," declared Rajasthan's Chief Minister Vasundhara Raje as she flew in to inaugurate it. Her helicopter circled the domed building before landing on the improvised

---

[1] *The UK Maharajahs: Inside the South Asian Success Story*, Nicholas Brealey Publishing.

helipad in a field next to the hospital. There was heavy security and it seemed as if the entire district administration had turned out to greet her. She emerged wearing a flame-coloured saree to greet my wife, Mohini, and me. The dust whirled round us, the air was scented with marigold from garlands and dozens of hands reached out to touch her, but despite the melee, she was her usual warm, friendly self. We had got to know her well over the past decade: first when she was the member of parliament for my ancestral home in Jhalawar district, and later when she became the Chief Minister of Rajasthan and moved to Jaipur. Her son, Raja Dushyant Singh, has taken over the baton from her in Jhalawar and is now our local member of parliament.

Bhawani Mandi is a tiny place that's barely even a dot on the map, and it has the dilemma of being located on the extreme edge of the state so that when the train stops at the local station half is in Rajasthan and half in Madhya Pradesh. Bhawani Mandi and Sunel are forever enshrined in my heart as places where my beloved mother presided over our happy holidays. That's where my father (before his premature death) and my grandfather built charitable institutions; and my mother, too, gifted several small homes to Sindhi refugees rendered homeless and penniless by the bloody Partition.

"Charitable work is my inheritance from my parents," I said in my speech at the hospital's inauguration. "If my grandfather could mortgage his family home to build a hospital here in the 1920s, then I can surely do better. And I'm not looking to make a profit from this hospital. Whatever income we generate in future will be ploughed back, to improve, to expand, and to update. My brothers and sisters of my ancestral hometown should have the best medical facilities."

Four thousand local people turned out for the inauguration that sunny morning and there was a carnival atmosphere. At the entrance to the hospital, Shrimati Vasundhara Raje cut the ceremonial red ribbon after being welcomed in the traditional manner by Mohini, who placed an auspicious red "tilak" mark on the Chief Minister's forehead. It was a happy and proud moment for me: my dream had turned into reality and I was surrounded by my family, my daughters, Zeenat and Zarmin, their husbands, Arun and Manraj, my granddaughter, Natania, my sisters, Ateka,

Shirin and Kaneez, my brothers, Abbasbhai and Akbar, their spouses, Moiz, Fakri and Rehanabhabhi, and several nieces and nephews. As soon as the Chief Minister cut the ribbon, we were swept into the hospital by the crowds, which is hard for anyone to imagine who has not experienced the effect that the presence of an Indian politician has on people. They swirled round the miniature model of the hospital kept at the entrance then virtually carried us into the large circular central lobby of the hospital with its elevated floor of marble inlay and its lofty dome soaring above it like a prayer to heaven.

The central lobby is dominated by a portrait of my mother. The accompanying plaque reads: "Paradise lies at the feet of the mother." My wife and I had commissioned the towering portrait from an artist in Udaipur when we visited that city two years earlier. The artist executed it from a photograph, a studio shot typical of the 1930s, black and white with colour filled in afterwards.

The hospital actually stands in isolation on the main road between Bhawani Mandi and Sunel but is well connected by bus to both. Easy access is important because the area is backward and poor. Surrounding villages get electricity for about two hours a day if they are wired up. School children can still be seen beneath the trees doing their lessons with chalk on slate. The hospital that my grandfather built eighty years ago, and which I have modernised, is still doing yeoman service but it's old. Unlike Delhi and Mumbai and other metropolitan cities that have world-class healthcare and have even become centres of medical tourism, the millions tiny *mofussil* towns and rural villages in which the bulk of Indians live offer basic, crude medical facilities. When I first dreamt up the idea of the hospital, everyone thought I was mad. But that's wasn't the first time – and it won't be the last! However, some like my good friend, Qaiser Shamim, Chief Commissioner of Income Tax for Haryana and his wife, Nahid, did encourage me in my plans and urged me to push ahead.

For years I had been repaying my ancestral land that gave me so much happiness in early life by building projects such as a sports stadium for college students, the local police station, a community centre for Harijans (formerly known as the Untouchable caste), and small rainwater dams called anikuts. Now I wanted to do something bigger and more meaningful that might help transform lives in a radical way: a modern hospital with state-of-the-art medical facilities.

My journey has always been essentially a solitary one, with people joining in along the way, and so it was with this hospital. Too ambitious! Who will use it? How will it be built, managed? Too expensive! Well, I put my own money where my mouth was and then I wheedled more out of friends such as Shaikh Mohammed Dadabhai of Bahrain, who has generously paid for one of the four wings. The first breakthrough came thanks to the Chief Minister, Mrs Raje, who gave me the plot of land for a nominal price

Then I conceptualised the design of the building, and with the help of Dr V. Desai and his company HOSMAC, who specialise in constructing and equipping hospitals, my dream became reality. I love building properties, whether they are charitable institutions or factories (I have probably constructed a dozen factories in my life). After the drawings, I had a model built to scale. Next, I hired a professional architect, Manoj Agarwal, experienced in constructing hospitals who survived the eccentricities of my endless demands as did my main contractor Mr Durga. He is from my own town Bhawani Mandi and as far as possible I used local workers and talent including tailors for the uniforms and linen, the contractor for the canteen and a special local bus service for the staff.

Old friends such as Sirish Shah of Mumbai helped enormously in resourcing and negotiating for equipment. The distinctive Kota stone we used came from the mines of Banas Stones in Jhalawar owned by Asad Anwar Khan – I have known three generations of his family. My legal adviser and friend, Ishwarchand Bhatnagar, and his son Vidhan have both been extremely helpful not only in the development of Noon Hospital but also in many aspects of my family's life in Bhawani Mandi. My own family members also gave invaluable help. My brother-in-law, Moiz Challawalla, made several trips to Bhawani Mandi from Mumbai over three years to oversee the project and even now still makes regular visits on my behalf; my daughter, Zeenat, and nephew, Nizar, made trips from London in the final stages to ensure that the hospital was ready for the opening.

Having lived and worked in London for the past forty years, I tend to apply British standards to projects, and so it was with the hospital. I have built modern, clean blocks of apartments for the medical and nursing staff. It's not easy to attract good doctors to remote rural areas and it helps to offer them good living accommodation. I took a lot of flak, even from the professional consultants, for insisting upon liberal use of marble and granite in the interiors. The central lobby, for example, has a large raised dais in the centre that is exquisitely inlaid with pale marble in dark green granite. The villagers, who are our patients, had seen nothing like it! But I am a firm believer that beautiful, aesthetic surroundings aid recovery. The Out Patients Department (OPD) is free of charge; 10 per cent of the beds are also free, and the rest will be charged according to patients' means.

The Chief Minister, in her stirring speech to the crowd, said:

> Don't think you won't be able to afford it. I know it looks like a palace or a five-star hotel, but it's meant for you. Don't be afraid to enter! The OPD is completely free. Some beds are also completely free. And there's something for everyone. There are general wards with six beds each, there are semi-private rooms with only two beds, and there are private rooms with one single bed. And they are with air conditioning and without air conditioning. And I took the opportunity to get my son's finger X-rayed: Raja hurt his finger whilst playing cricket and I'm anxious to know if he has hurt it badly. I'm waiting for the result of the X-ray – so you see I'm the first one to use the hospital. My son is its first patient.

The crowd that had gathered must have taken the message to heart for on its very first full day thirty-five patients visited the OPD. By day five, the number had swelled to sixty-five.

It gave me such satisfaction to survey the rows of men in colourful Rajasthani turbans and the women in their sarees gathered there, as well as a large contingent of white-clad Bohras from my own community and their wives in light-coloured burkhas. The day before the inauguration, we held three short religious blessings with priests from the major Indian faiths of Hinduism, Islam and Sikhism at a small function attended by a handful of invitees. India is truly a secular country where all religions are embraced and I have a tradition of getting a new venture anointed by different priests. I couldn't help adding in my speech, "If someone had told me years back that I would be sitting next to the Chief Minister to dedicate a hospital to the service of the people of Bhawani Mandi and Sunel, I wouldn't have believed it!"

After the inauguration the Chief Minister took off in her helicopter again but everyone else stayed on to drink tea and coffee and eat snacks, including the Indian sweets that are considered auspicious and hence indispensable for joyous occasions. Half an hour later the skies opened and it poured down, an uncharacteristic shower for that time of year. Rain, they say, is lucky and a good omen (although it was followed by a terrific hailstorm). On top of that, honey bees were found nesting in one corner of the hospital roof. Another good omen!

As it is laden with such good luck, I'm confident that the hospital will succeed. Two more wings need to be built before the whole complex is complete. My dream is that we will be able to offer a self-contained medical service there carrying out everything from critical eye operations (eye disease is a big issue for so many Indians) to heart operations. But somehow I feel I have fulfilled the promise to both my father and my mother that I made all those years ago beside my father's death bed. I knew my immediate family were taken care of, but I had an extended family at home in Sunel and Bhawani Mandi and my duty to them was just as powerful. So, as well as being practical for the villagers – more than 500 patients attended a recent open day we organised – the hospital is also symbolic for me. As I write this, the hospital is full, the third wing has been built and will be inaugurated in January 2009.

I travel between Bhawani Mandi and London three or four times a year and every time I am back in India I am stunned by the speed of change. Not only is the infrastructure being transformed but I am delighted to say attitudes are moving forward just as fast. On my last visit for example I met in my own district two young female politicians, Aruna Meena and Nitu Verma, who both hold important positions in public life; such a thing would have been unheard of ten years ago. Both are highly educated and that is exactly what India needs if it is really to modernise its political system.

As every Indian is aware, the biggest curse on their country is corruption; there seems to be a scam at almost every level and it is up to the young politicians, collectors and civil servants who are just moving into positions of authority to rid the country of this practice.

★ ★ ★

However, the fire still burns in my belly as fiercely as it did on the day when I left my home as a lad with big dreams. The family, my extended clan, have been taken care of, the business I managed to grow with the help of so many people has fulfilled even my wildest ambitions – but the energy remains. So the question stands: what next?

List of Appointments

2006   Watford & Northwest Business Person of the Year Award
Zee Telefilms Ltd – independent director
Pravasi Bharativa Samman Award – Gold Medal presented by
President of India, APJ Abdul Kalam
Good Relations (India) Pvt Ltd – board member

2005   Bridges Community Ventures Ltd – non-executive director
Honorary Life Vice President Surrey County Cricket Club
Casualty Plus Limited – non-executive director
Kingston University – Honorary Degree of Doctor of Business
Administration

2004   Obento Limited (Subway Restaurants) – non-executive director
NeutraHealth Plc – non executive director
Home Office – member of Advisory Board on Naturalisation and
Integration
Britain in Europe – director
Asian Business Award for community service in the UK and India
Transport for London – Board member appointed by Mayor of
London

2003   Sage Business Awards (in conjunction with *The Daily Telegraph*) –
winner of "Best Business Leader" award in the category of
100+ employees
Asian Jewel Awards – South of Britain Lifetime Achievement
Award

2002 Carlton Television – Multicultural Achievement Award for
Outstanding Contribution to British Business
Middlesex University – Honorary Degree of Doctor of the
University
Knight Bachelor – Sir Gulam Noon conferred by Her Majesty
Queen Elizabeth II
Care International UK – Board member
London Chamber of Commerce & Industry – President
University of Central England Birmingham – Honorary Degree of
Doctor of the University
Cancer Research UK – founder member

2001 London Guildhall University – Honorary Degree of Doctor of
Business Administration

2000 Ethnic Minority Business Forum – member

1999 The British Food Trust – trustee

1998 University of Surrey – Honorary Degree of Master of the University
Memorial Gates Trust – Trustee

1996 Arpana Charitable Trust UK – trustee
Member of the Order of the British Empire (MBE)
The Advisory Council of The Prince's Trust – member

1995 Covent Garden Market Authority – Board director
Noon Group – chairman
Asian Business Association – founder and chairman
Noon Foundation – Trustee and chairman of the Trust Board

1994 Asian of the Year

1988 Noon Products Ltd (now part of Kerry Foods Ltd) – founder and
chairman

1972 Bombay Halwa Ltd – founder, chairman and managing director

Index of Names